Harris's list of Covent-Garden ladies: or man of pleasure's kalendar, for the year 1773. Containing an exact description of the most celebrated ladies of pleasure ...

Harris

PRINT EDITIONS

Eighteenth Century
Collections Online
Print Editions

Gale ECCO Print Editions

Relive history with *Eighteenth Century Collections Online*, now available in print for the independent historian and collector. This series includes the most significant English-language and foreign-language works printed in Great Britain during the eighteenth century, and is organized in seven different subject areas including literature and language; medicine, science, and technology; and religion and philosophy. The collection also includes thousands of important works from the Americas.

The eighteenth century has been called "The Age of Enlightenment." It was a period of rapid advance in print culture and publishing, in world exploration, and in the rapid growth of science and technology – all of which had a profound impact on the political and cultural landscape. At the end of the century the American Revolution, French Revolution and Industrial Revolution, perhaps three of the most significant events in modern history, set in motion developments that eventually dominated world political, economic, and social life.

In a groundbreaking effort, Gale initiated a revolution of its own: digitization of epic proportions to preserve these invaluable works in the largest online archive of its kind. Contributions from major world libraries constitute over 175,000 original printed works. Scanned images of the actual pages, rather than transcriptions, recreate the works *as they first appeared.*

Now for the first time, these high-quality digital scans of original works are available via print-on-demand, making them readily accessible to libraries, students, independent scholars, and readers of all ages.

For our initial release we have created seven robust collections to form one the world's most comprehensive catalogs of 18th century works.

Initial Gale ECCO Print Editions collections include:

History and Geography
Rich in titles on English life and social history, this collection spans the world as it was known to eighteenth-century historians and explorers. Titles include a wealth of travel accounts and diaries, histories of nations from throughout the world, and maps and charts of a world that was still being discovered. Students of the War of American Independence will find fascinating accounts from the British side of conflict.

Social Science

Delve into what it was like to live during the eighteenth century by reading the first-hand accounts of everyday people, including city dwellers and farmers, businessmen and bankers, artisans and merchants, artists and their patrons, politicians and their constituents. Original texts make the American, French, and Industrial revolutions vividly contemporary.

Medicine, Science and Technology

Medical theory and practice of the 1700s developed rapidly, as is evidenced by the extensive collection, which includes descriptions of diseases, their conditions, and treatments. Books on science and technology, agriculture, military technology, natural philosophy, even cookbooks, are all contained here.

Literature and Language

Western literary study flows out of eighteenth-century works by Alexander Pope, Daniel Defoe, Henry Fielding, Frances Burney, Denis Diderot, Johann Gottfried Herder, Johann Wolfgang von Goethe, and others. Experience the birth of the modern novel, or compare the development of language using dictionaries and grammar discourses.

Religion and Philosophy

The Age of Enlightenment profoundly enriched religious and philosophical understanding and continues to influence present-day thinking. Works collected here include masterpieces by David Hume, Immanuel Kant, and Jean-Jacques Rousseau, as well as religious sermons and moral debates on the issues of the day, such as the slave trade. The Age of Reason saw conflict between Protestantism and Catholicism transformed into one between faith and logic -- a debate that continues in the twenty-first century.

Law and Reference

This collection reveals the history of English common law and Empire law in a vastly changing world of British expansion. Dominating the legal field is the *Commentaries of the Law of England* by Sir William Blackstone, which first appeared in 1765. Reference works such as almanacs and catalogues continue to educate us by revealing the day-to-day workings of society.

Fine Arts

The eighteenth-century fascination with Greek and Roman antiquity followed the systematic excavation of the ruins at Pompeii and Herculaneum in southern Italy; and after 1750 a neoclassical style dominated all artistic fields. The titles here trace developments in mostly English-language works on painting, sculpture, architecture, music, theater, and other disciplines. Instructional works on musical instruments, catalogs of art objects, comic operas, and more are also included.

The BiblioLife Network

This project was made possible in part by the BiblioLife Network (BLN), a project aimed at addressing some of the huge challenges facing book preservationists around the world. The BLN includes libraries, library networks, archives, subject matter experts, online communities and library service providers. We believe every book ever published should be available as a high-quality print reproduction; printed on-demand anywhere in the world. This insures the ongoing accessibility of the content and helps generate sustainable revenue for the libraries and organizations that work to preserve these important materials.

The following book is in the "public domain" and represents an authentic reproduction of the text as printed by the original publisher. While we have attempted to accurately maintain the integrity of the original work, there are sometimes problems with the original work or the micro-film from which the books were digitized. This can result in minor errors in reproduction. Possible imperfections include missing and blurred pages, poor pictures, markings and other reproduction issues beyond our control. Because this work is culturally important, we have made it available as part of our commitment to protecting, preserving, and promoting the world's literature.

GUIDE TO FOLD-OUTS MAPS and OVERSIZED IMAGES

The book you are reading was digitized from microfilm captured over the past thirty to forty years. Years after the creation of the original microfilm, the book was converted to digital files and made available in an online database.

In an online database, page images do not need to conform to the size restrictions found in a printed book. When converting these images back into a printed bound book, the page sizes are standardized in ways that maintain the detail of the original. For large images, such as fold-out maps, the original page image is split into two or more pages

Guidelines used to determine how to split the page image follows:

• Some images are split vertically; large images require vertical and horizontal splits.
• For horizontal splits, the content is split left to right.
• For vertical splits, the content is split from top to bottom.
• For both vertical and horizontal splits, the image is processed from top left to bottom right.

1 June. Im Sculp

HARRIS's LIST

OF

Covent-Garden Ladies:

OR

MAN OF PLEASURE's

KALENDAR,

For the YEAR 1773.

CONTAINING

An exact Description of the most celebrated Ladies of Pleasure who frequent COVENT-GARDEN, and other
Parts of this Metropolis.

LONDON:

Printed for H. RANGER, Temple-Ex-
change Passage, Fleet-Street.

MDCCLXXIII.

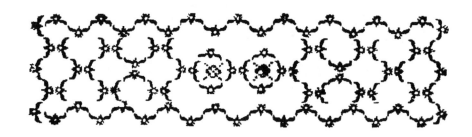

CONTENTS.
1773

Q

HARRIS's LIST

OF THE

COVENT GARDEN LADIES.

Mrs. Haines, *alias* Windfor. *Glafs fhop in Marquis Court.*

How low finks beauty when by vice debas'd.

THERE are few forms, if we may be allowed to give our opinion, that pleafe us more than this lady, fhe is about that fize the poets and painters depict the Queen of Love, her features are foft and pleafing, her face a beautiful oval, rather too thin (but a late mifcarriage, we fuppofe, may have occafioned it) her eyes blue, her hair light, her fkin, even envy muft allow, but feldom equalled, upon the whole, fhe is a woman, we fhould imagine, would give general fatisfaction, yet fo capricious are appetites in men, that this lady has often (when

B

we

we have thought to have conferred a favour by introducing her) been rejected for one whofe only recommendation (like fome ladies lap-dogs) muft certainly have been her uglinefs: however we muft allow Providence is very impartial in her gifts; fhe gave this lady beauty and thought that enough. She lived fome time in private with a gentleman in the city, from thence removed to Mrs. Pen—they's in Bow Street, then to Lucy Cooper's, and now, having a tolerable fet of acquaintance, trades upon her own bottom, and, poor girl, is dying at this time for Capt. L—y, in the Kings Bench, for whofe heart there are many competitors.

Mifs Grafton. *Bow Street Covent Garden*

She's more than mortal that ne'er err'd at all.

We have more than once mentioned our impartiality, and we can affure our readers that nothing can or fhall prevail upon us to deviate from it. Affection or intereft fhall have no fway or bias with us. The tafk we have undertaken obliges us to be impartial, and the public may be fatisfied that thro' the whole of this performance we fhall
ftictly

ftictly adhere to truth as far as we can get to the knowledge of it , and that we fhall entirely follow our own opinion in the characters we give : if they may not tally with thofe of our readers, we hope they will do us the juftice to believe that we write divefted of all prejudice either for or againft the parties.

We are well aware how many enemies we fhall make ourfelves, for even the lovelieft character in the lift will not think herfelf done juftice by What have we then to expect from the reft ? When every lady has beautifying glaffes at her toilet and fees herfelf in no other, they will not allow that their optics are untrue they will not allow that men fee with different eyes to theirs . but however, pleafe or not pleafe, we have this confolation, that we have pur-fued impaitiality and given our opinion as things really appeared to us.

We have thought proper to place this preface before this character as we know our fentiments of this lady will be thought by fome not to do her juftice; thofe gentleman will pleafe to remember, we have paffed the hey-day of our blood and do not fee with lovers eyes, the mift has been long removed from ours.

and

and things appear to us in their real ſtate.

Miſs Grafton has been conſidered by many as one of the fineſt women on town: by ſome as the *fineſt*. we allow ſhe is pretty, a good figure, ſparkling eyes, her features ſmall and pleaſing, and her ſhape genteel; yet we cannot think her the complete beauty, much, very much is wanted to form it——'tis not a lip, an eye, a cheek—'tis a juſt and pleaſing aſſemblage of the whole, yet moſt authors allow there never was ſuch a being——perfection is not in nature— for our part we are of their opinion; what pleaſes one diſguſts another—ſome chuſe fair hair, others black, ſome blue eyes, others brown——who then ſhall fix the criterion? But to return: had this lady as many more perfections of *body* as ſhe already poſſeſſes, ſhe would not by any means be the lady we ſhould ſelect for our amuſement, there is ſomething that recommends much ſtronger than beauty, and which this lady poſſeſſes but a very moderate ſhare of. That bubble, Vanity, has ſo elated her that *ſelf* alone engroſſes all her thoughts, and little I, the heroine of the tale, is ſure eternally to be her table talk.   She

She is said to be sister to Miss Betsy
Mo...on, how true we know not, there
goes not appear to us any likeness either
in person manners, but mothers have
had two children as much unlike witness
Eve, in Cain and Abel—we leave our
reader to make whatever application he
thinks proper: should it be an ill natured one, we hope it will not be laid
to our charge.

Miss Grafton is also a competitor for
the heart of that *amiable man* Capt L—y,
in the King's Bench; she had an amour,
of some time standing, with a Mr.
Foll—t, but we hope his eyes are open.
A woman of her cast is hardly worth
notice unless for mere amusement, no
intimate acquaintance or connexion
should be made with her, as she is
well known to have as *tender a regard* for
the male part of the sex, as a wolf or a
lamb—a cheating attorney, for his
client—or mother—. for the health of
her customers, by selling such infernal
liquors—a poor ignorant Irishman, piping
hot arrived, fell into her clutches and
she fleeced the poor devil so much that
she scarce left him a coat to his back,
and insolently laughed at him in prison
where he was confined for debts contrac'ed
for

for her ufe : fhe may be found at the Cat in the Strand, almoft every evening, and fometimes at the Blakeney's-head in Bow-ftreet, tho' this houfe is not calculated for that lady, as they there preferve decency and good order.

*Mrs.*Blake. *Martlet-Court, Covent Garden.*

Good language join'd with inoffenfive wit.

Our firft acquaintance with this lady was when fhe was fervant maid to the rib of Capt. D- R-, in the King's Bench, here fhe formed a connexion with the gentleman whofe name fhe bears, by whom fhe has had two children, fhe was moftly with him in the Bench (as he alfo was a prifoner) but her leifure hours fhe gave to us, having taken up her refidence for that purpofe as above. She is about the middling fize, plump—three or four-and-twenty, light hair, tolerable good fkin, and tho' low her origin, yet behaves extremely well and is much efteemed in company. we have juft heard fhe has entirely taken up with her fwain, who lives in the rules of the Bench, in Blackman ftreet—but fhould curiofity prompt any of our readers, as Walpole fays— Every one have their price.

Mifs

Miss Thompson. *At a Barber's, in the Hay-market.*

Ne'er wants something pertinent to say.

This lady lived a twelve-month with Mr. B—, in the Kings Bench, whom we mentioned to have made a connexion with Capt. R—'s maid. She is a very fine figure, walks well, has a good face and neck, and a remarkable fall of the shoulders; brown hair, about two-and-twenty years of age, florid complexion, and has a little stammering in her speech: she will now-and-then break loose, but we have all our faults, and Miss Thompson none but such as may be easily forgiven. We would recommend it to her not to be too frequent in her visits to the King's Bench; but like several other fine women she studies to obtain what will never be worth her trouble when she has it—a *Hart.*

Miss Cotton, *alias* White, *alias* Balford. *Berner street.*

True, she is fair oh! how divinely fair.

Miss Balford (for that is her real name, being the daughter of a tradesman in Bride-lane, Fleet-street) however young
she

she may appear, has been numbered amongst the nymphs of Venus three years. Her skin exceeds even the whiteness of enamel, her lovely blue eyes, the halcyon's azure plume, her every feature is an excitement to love, her figure, tho' short, is pleasing, and formed with the greatest symmetry and proportion · she may well be called a happy acquisition to the sisterhood, but we hear she has left us to live in private; however great the loss we sustain, we are never more happy than when we can with a lady joy of so valuable a situation. We hope she will remember she will not always be young

Miss S—ls. In King Street, Covent Garden.

" *The passion love unto their fancy brings*"
" *The prettiest notions and the softest things.*"

These ladies have so long figured in private that they might arraign us of partiality if we did not *honor* them with a place. 'Tis true, they have often favoured us with their company, and 'twas with secret pleasure we have beheld them when we have had the honor to wait behind their chairs at our house, with how much composure
they

they have stood the most indecent attacks made upon their persons and understandings; our brother Robinson * had often remarked his agreeable neighbours to us, when they lived in Katherine Street, and their father kept a silversmith and jeweller's shop, a poor old German, whose heart they broke, and he, in a fit of insanity, tied himself up in his garters, when they lodged in Great Queen Street, after having left their house in the aforesaid street. After his death they removed to the house they now inhabit in King Street, with their aged mother, who, poor woman, is no more than a cypher, having no will of her own, being obliged to her daughters for her support; she answers, however, their ends, and I suppose they find it to their purpose to give her victuals, or else they are so good œconomists the old lady would long ago have been sent to the workhouse.

Were we to enumerate half their intrigues since their commencement, it would

---

* A pimp at the Fountain in Katherine Street.

would fill two pretty novels for Mr. Noble's Library, and therefore much exceed the bounds of our work: the eldest of them is a good shewy girl, rather going down hill, she has, to be sure, gone thro' a good deal of service and taken some rough medicines to cause abortion, which have pretty much affected her, yet notwithstanding we give her the preference.

The youngest is not so tall as her sister, her complexion somewhat better, for the good girl let Nature take its course and has a fine daughter, who lives at home with them, tho' under the sanction of a young lady as a boarder. The eldest cannot be less than thirty, the other, perhaps, three years younger. They are good company, and indeed not despicable as to understanding they have seen a good deal of the town, and can superficially talk on most subjects, but the theatre is their favourite. If our readers will call, when sauntering by their shop, and buy a trifle, they will allow part of what we have said to be true, and a present, well timed, and a jaunt into the country will make them acquainted with all their *secrets*.

N. E.

N. B. They underſtand jilting, and will fight ſhy a long time, a coup de maitre will therefore be neceſſary.

Mrs. Williams. *Plough Court, Fetter-Lane.*

" *Modeſtly Bold.*"

Mrs Williams, an old crony of the celebrated tally woman Judith Veale, has got the length of the foot of a mercer on Ludgate-hill, and keeps her maid and houſe and indeed to appearrance lives very comfortable, her neighbours are apprized of her connexion and therefore wonder much at ſeeing a handſome young fellow frequently pay her viſits in the day, for her keeper's hour is after five, ſo that, when his wife (for he is married) imagines him gone to the coffee-houſe. Yet notwithſtanding we have a few more on our Liſt, to thoſe gentlemen who would come at our feaſting we ſhall have always know our men of ſpirit, ſo know the trouble under theſe matters. There is nothing elſe in it if the price is rather plain, but it will be genuine and agreeable even if ſhe is in circumſtances, her ſons is very good and away late, and we thoſe things will
wit

what she gets from her keeper and the odd guineas she makes at times with us, she might save money, but her acquaintance, we are afraid will never let her grow rich. We are sorry to say we have often seen her come home so intoxicated as not to be able to stand, to the no small entertainment of her neighbours : she should reflect upon the ill consequences both as to her health and purse, and the ravages it must make in both the one and the other. The common excuse of women of the town she cannot make use of · want never pinches her, and therefore she has no occasion for the care dispelling glass ; we beg to recommend sobriety to her, as her chains would easily be broken if once discovered in a drunken fit.--Shameful in a man—most abominable in a women.

Mrs. Steers. *Brownlow Street, Holborn.*

" *The vices common to her sex can find*
" *No room, e'en in the suburb of her mind* "

Mrs. Steers took her name from a Broker in the city with whom she lived some time in Warwick-Court Holborn ; she was brought up a millener with her
aunt,

aunt, who lives in Cornhill, and was actually seduced from home by one of her own sex who initiated her into the mysteries of Venus: she is really a pretty figure, and has a handsome face with good features; she was a good while upon the public, but as we have not seen her lately with us, believe she is in keeping with a Jew, with whom she was in the boxes at the play. This lady declares against the joys of love— she says, she finds none of that exquisite delight that women talk of with such rapture: but whether her declaration be true or not we cannot say, but if true, her eyes give her heart the lye.

Miss Nancy B-gn-ll. *Knightsbridge.*

" *Soft as the wild ducks tender young*
" *That float on Avon's tide,*
" *Bright as the water lilly sprung,*
" *And glittering by its side* "

Nancy Bignell was brought up a French trimming maker and very early discovered a strong propensity to Venus she commenced, in her fifteenth year (four years since) and has lived with one gentleman the whole time, which we much wonder at, as she is not possessed

C   of

of art fufficient to manage a lover, and her Strephon is of the moft fickle pro-feffion—an officer.

She is a ftraight, fine made girl, and lovely as the morn, her every motion is an excitement to love, her eyes beat to arms and her fnowy bofom fummonfes you to furrender; if beauty and artlefs fimplicity could retain the heart of man, we think Nancy might well hope to enjoy her lover, but alas! we know our own fex and are no ftrangers to its vice: .he moft conftant of us are fickle crea-tures indeed!

Mrs. F-wl-r. No. 10, *Langthorne-Couit,*
Coleman Street.

" *On every youth her favour throws.*"

This lady is the daughter of a tavern keeper who formerly refided clofe to the New Church in the Strand. her uncle dying and leaving her about a thoufand pounds, fhe began, at a very early age, to think herfelf a woman and look out for a hufland: a young fellow, a hofier, and juft out of his time (without a fhil-ling) paid his addreffes and carried his point: as foon as fhe had thrown off the trammels her parents had laid upon her,

her, she shewd her inclinations without reserve—he took a shop next the India-house, in Leadenhall Street, where Madam's pride was gratified, by the continual resort of Turks, Jews and Infidels, who paid her the most fulsome compliments. Jemmy was quite contented, as it brought grist to his mill, and Madam was mightily pleased as she partook of every diversion offered her, and often has mounted her horse with her *Cicisbeo* at her husband's own door, however in a short time she complimented her *Dearee* with a very fashionable disorder, and so matters came to an open rupture—he swore, and she swore—and so told they the story to all that came to the shop—Her friends began to look shy, but having a good constitution she did not shew it, and in a short time got entirely rid of it. Her fame is well known about the Change and Lombard Street—at last poor Mr. F-wl-r found business very sensibly decay and was obliged to make up his affairs with a bankruptcy, after which he set out for India, where it is said he is making hasty strides to be a Nabob.

Madam now took her full swing of pleasure, and openly avowed it, she

lived

lived fome time with Mr. Alderman
Rawl—n, the Grocer; at prefent fhe is
in keeping with a Sweet Youth, a Sugar
Baker, in Thames Street, who is fitting
up a houfe in his own neighbourhood for
her reception. She is of a middle fize,
good fkin, very plump, but not fat, has
a remarkable fhort nofe, good hair and
fine eyes, and 'tis reported, by way of
compleating her armorous character, that
fhe is not unacquainted with thofe ma-
rœuvres in bed which give fuch exquifite
delight.

Mifs Kitty W-ll-s, *alias* D---e. *Cumberland-Court.*

" *In every Gefture dignity and Love.*"

This lady was born of Englifh parents, at Bruffels; fpeaks very good
French, has a natural gaiety of temper,
genteel in her deportment and behaviour
—does not want for underftanding however ill fhe may apply it. She is much
indebted both to beauty and fortune, to
the former for a very lovely fkin, beautiful eyes, of a dark brown, fine carna-
tion in her cheeks, a lovely pair of pouting lips, fine teeth, an agreeable fore-
head, and dark brown hair. Some pre
tend

tend to say she is too lusty, but 'tis not
our province to determine in these matters, we only give things as they are,
and to the best of our knowledge, im-
partially. To fortune she is indebted
for many wealthy keepers, tho' indeed
her beauty might well demand them.
The late Marquis of Tavistock bestow-
ed his favours on her in a princely manner, to him succeeded Eden (an Officer
in the East India service) but her extravagance exceeded even his immoderate
love for her, and from the Fleet, where
she was some time confined and lived
nobly, as numbers who experienced her
bounty there can testify (for good nature
is her foible) she removed to Marquis-
Court, where she sat up a Jelly-shop,
there she met another lover, fond and
bountiful as her last; but Drake did not
long enjoy this fair one, death put a period to his love and her support—here
she began an acquaintance with—*Want*,
her creditors grew clamorous, no words
would satisfy them, and the Marshalsea
was soon her lot; her creditors, however
relented, grew pliable, and in ten
weeks gave her her discharge, well
judging that to enable her to pay her
debts she must have her liberty. She is

just

juft emerged from her confinement, and we hope will avoid the rock fhe has fo often fplit on. There is one thing in her aftonifhing, this is, her uncommon deteftation of her keepers, however agreeable , and the plundering of them to fupport another man whofe only recommendation, perhaps, is that of wanting every good quality of head and heart, and has only poverty to plead in his favour.

Madam M-n-fi-re.

" *Too fine a dancer for a Virtuous Woman.*"

This lady's figure is too well known to need our defcription, we have only mentioned her to acquaint our readers (who chufe to go to her price) that fhe is comeatable. Her keeper, about three years fince, ufed frequently to make her undergo the difcipline of the horfewhip to reftrain her to what he thought good fubjection. A Dancer at the fame Theatre has pinned himfelf upon her fleeve, but like a true Frenchman, will hold the candle (fhould his prefence be neceflary) or leave the room at any time to make way for his betters. She fpeaks

English

Englifh pretty well, and is a tolerable good companion.

Mrs. E-m-nds, *alias* W-ll--ms. *Cheefe-monger's, Church Street, Soho.*

" *To gold and pewifhnefs inclin'd.*"

A tall fine figure. She lived fome time at the Parrot facing Beaufort Buildings in the Strand, which fhe opened as a Milliner's Shop—a mere cloak to her more private bufinefs. A few yards of ribbon and a gauze apron thrown over a line in the window confituting her whole merchandize, at leaft of that kind fhe now is at a warehoufe as above. She is a tall, black woman, by fome faid to be a fine woman, but we think coarfe: fhe is now faid to be in good keeping, but any one who is curious may have her, for fhe is fond of money, fo very fond, that fhe never was known to turn even half a crown away—'tis true fhe is made to go thro' a good deal of *hard work*, and 'tis thought by all her acquaintance fhe is feldom idle, tho' in keeping, her drefs is always elegant, and yet fhe may be found moft nights in the gallery at Covent Garden.

N. B. Right hand corner.

Mifs

Miſs W-ll -n-on. *At* Mrs *Pl-dw-ll's, the*
c'. of Long-Acre Bagnio.

" Ten c cıſand pounds for an ınch more "

This girl has been ſome time in the
country with a gentleman, who is very
fond of her, and now returned for the
winter to her former lodging, ſhe is
rather ſhort, thin and fair, and of that
kind of diſpoſition that ſhe can enjoy,
to exceſs, every male object that comes
in her way; the calves of her legs
are greatly exhauſted by her inſatiable
appetite to venery, ſhe is great'y troubled
with a diſorder incident to the fair x,
called the fluor albus, and as a Iriſh
Clergyman uſed to ſay of Peg. Woffing-
ton, with whom he uſed to pray—" by
" Jeſus, go when you-will to her—, it is
" like a puppy-dog's noſe, cold and
-" wet."—However, upon the whole, ſhe
is not a bad piece to thoſe who are not
over delicate, and don't mind a little
ſlip-ſlop-work.

Miſs.

Miſs D-ſ-n.　*At Mr. Robinſon's, in King Street, Soho.*

" *Ever good natured, always kind,*
" *Willing to pleaſe, ever in the mind."*

This lady is remarkable for her good humour, and condeſcenſion, were ſhe even ugly, one could not help being pleaſed with her, thro' that ſweetneſs of temper which ſhe poſſeſſes; ſhe ſcarcely ever ſays no to any thing, but on the contrary, alwaysaſſents her perſon is genteel, of a fair complexion, and delightful hair, her paſſion for the ſport ſeems fine to be guided by reaſon, and medium ſeems to be preſerved throughout her whole conduct. A very fit girl to be taken off the town, as ſhe would be an agreeable companion and capable of leading a rational life, in being proof againſt incontinence. The God of Love ſeems to have intended a better fate for her charms, than proſtitution, at the hazard of all that is dear to her.

Charlotte Benevent.　*Princes Street, the Corner of Liſle Street, Leiceſter-Fields.*

,, *Novelty has 'its charms to pleaſe."*

This lady was born in Holland, but ſpeaks French and Engliſh tolerably well, the she is of the middle stature, fine black eyes, and eye brows, dresses in an elegant taste and seldom goes out, having a set of particular acquaintance who enable her to live somewhat above the common rate. Above, on the second floor, lodges Miss Boothby, mentioned in our last year's, with whom she has no connection, thinking herself much superior to any in a second floor, and who is continually pading of it, to seek for customers, her price is one pound one, from a person she likes, but otherwise she must be paid like a foreigner and *a woman of uncommon discernment.*

Mrs. M-xfi-ld. *At a Taylor's, facing the White House in Rupert Street, St. Ann's.*

"She melts in his arms and give a loose to joy."

A fine tall agreeable woman, plump, clear complexion, expressive and very good natured, her eyes claim attention and entreat for what she enjoys most extravagantly, she requires but little importunity from a young fellow she thinks capable of performing his part well; money seems to be of no other use to her than the means of supplying
the

the neceſſary recruits of Nature with their former vig ir She is ſo ſkilful that ſhe never contracts any diſorder, always taking care to examine her man before he com to action. No price is fixt upon his pocket here, provided he pleaſes on the contrary, if he is very active in the ſport and comes on properly and repeatedly, he may be welcome to her bed wherever ſhe is not particularly engaged, even then, unleſs the caſh runs very low, ſhe will prefer her favorite and give denial to the fond fool who would pay her well.

Mrs. L-w-s. No. 11 Market Row Portland Street.

" *Happy is he who ſhuns the road to filth.*"

Here is a lady who ſeldom refuſes any man who has the appearance of wearing a crown in his pocket, as ſhe is agreeable without much meaning, and perhaps conſcious of her ſmall degree of perfection, ſhe contents herſelf with quick returns of ſmall ſums, and to ſay the truth ſuch cuſtom ſhe has in the ſmall way, that ſhe clears at leaſt two or three pounds a week, ſhe never looſes a cuſtomer but when ghnorrhea ſimplex keeps

him

him from her lodging, which now-and-
then is the cafe, tho' he makes ufe of
all the precaution poffible—but who can
withftand the power of numbers?

Mifs B--dg-m-n, alas Mrs. B-ll-rd.
Lately lodged at Mrs. Parker's, in Bull-
and-Mouth Street

" *Boldly fhe ventures to the feat of blifs.*"

A fmall genteel girl, with good fea-
tures-we cannot call this lady a beauty
of the firft clafs, fhe is what may be
reckoned pretty, but nothing extraordinary, and tho' fhe cannot boaft of fo
many external graces as many others,
yet I have been told, when fhe is engaged in her bufinefs, there are very
few who equal her. She is amorous to
a great degree, fearing not the largeft
or ftrongeft man that ever drew his
weapon in the caufe.

Mifs S—rt   At Mr. F—d's, in Church
Street, St. Ann's.

·" *If to her fhare fome female errors fall*
·" *Look on her face and you'll forget em' all.*"

This lady may be called a fine girl,
having a regular fet of features, fair
                                    complexion,

complexion, good-natured, and an honeſt open countenance. She was debauched by a young officer, who was the cauſe of her quitting her parents, perſons of un-doubted character, as ſhop - keepers, about twenty miles from London, who would, at this time, have given almoſt any thing they are poſſeſſed of, for her to return home ; but, the ſituation ſhe is in being known in the neighbourhood, ſhe is determined to undergo any diſtreſs or misfortune, rather than go home again. With this reſolution ſhe abandons herſelf to the Cyprian Deity, and is likely to be favoured under his auſpices.

Miſs Sm—h.   *At Mr. Carrol's, Taviſtock Row.*

　" *Cold as the ice itſelf,*
　" *She admires nought but pelf.*"

This lady is tall, and remarkably well made; her eyes are captivating, and have much expreſſion , add to this, a ſet of incomparable good teeth, renders her a very ſtriking object.   She has all the allure that a girl of trade can poſſibly be poſſeſſed of, ſhe can wheedle and coax the moſt penurious man out of his caſh. Where impotence has taken place, with

D　　　　　a ma-a manual operation, she can raise the dead to life, and if nature should prove deficient in the very act of sensation, she will tip you the exquisites in such a manner, as will make your vigour return afresh: cool in her own passion, her study is to give as much satisfaction to her man as possible: trying every method to please, and stir up Hymen's torch, is what she thinks her duty, and, like many of the French women of pleasure, abandons herself totally to your fancy: but, when her business is done, she expects a genteel and prompt payment, both which no one should grudge, for really she is indefatigable.

Mrs. H—n-ri-ge. *Moorfields.*

" *Like Heav'n, she takes no pleasure to destroy.*"

Sister-in-law to a lady in these lists, named F-wl-r, whose brother she married, unfortunately for him, for the poor fellow scarce ever after knew what happiness was. He got madam with child before the ceremony, as she says; and thereon she went to his house, (a brassfounder in Houndsditch), and insisted upon not quitting it, alledging it was her's,

her's, and that she would remain where-
ever he was   Her friends by promising
him a sum of money, (which they never
gave him) made up the match.   She
launched out into all the fashionable fol-
lies, and soon melted all her husband's
brass into caps, handkerchiefs and aprons,
he became a bankrupt, and she has sent
him into the country to his relations to
graze, that she might take her swing of
pleasure more uncontrouled.

She is not so lusty as her sister F-w-l-r,
whom we have mentioned, a little pock-
marked genteel, tho' not handsome,
and has a neat leg and foot, her hair
light-coloured, and her eyes grey.   She
has a good deal of life and spirits in
company, and is agreeable and chatty.

Her sister and she always hunt together, and may be often met with at the
bread and butter manufactories at Isling-
ton, but more especially at White-Con-
duit House, with the master of which
Mrs. Fowler had an intrigue.   As they
are of quite different make, there seem,
policy in their being together, as they
cannot interfere with each other's swains,
and it answers several other purposes,
which they know well to turn to their advantage.

We

We wish they would not endeavour at the dress of the ladies in the Strand, with such bunches of ribbons, such tawdry dresses, and boldness in their countenances. If they mean to have citizens for their admirers, their very looks are enough to frighten them from beginning a conversation.

Miss C--nfi-ld. *New Buildings, Marybone.*

> " *View but those nymphs that other swains*
> *adore,*
> " *You'd value charming Cr-nfi-ld still the*
> *more.*"

Miss Cr-nfi-ld is the daughter of a German lady now in the King's Bench for debt. She is said to be a German baroness, but what right she has to that title, we will not take upon us to determine, our business is with her daughter, who is undoubtedly a very fine woman. She is full six feet high, her hair a fine flaxen, her skin good, her eyes grey, and her features in general very pretty. She has been some time from her mother with a beloved Strephon, whose acquaintance she made when her mother was in the Marshalsea, before she removed to where she now is. How eligible her
choice

choice we will not pretend to fay. We cannot help thinking but her mother muſt be privy to her amours, as ſhe is continually backwards and forwards to ſee her, and has no other view of ſupport than what ſhe receives from the generous public, to whom ſhe has for ſome time diſpoſed of her favours, but at an extravagant price, though indeed only what her charms might well demand.

Miſs H-ll. *At Mrs. Thornton's under the Piazza.*

——— " *her charms wou'd move* " *Old age and frozen impotence to love.*"

A pretty delicate little girl, but rather too low in her behaviour, but this may be owing to living in the houſe where ſhe now reſides. Her hair is brown, her eyes very pleaſing, her ſkin remarkably white, her ſtature ſhort, and rather ſlim, but plump. She lately indeed ſuffered from an engagement with the enemy, and was obliged to be *hove down,* but her *leaks* are all ſtopt, and the carpenters have reported her tight and fit for ſervice. She is now on a cruize, and we wiſh her ſucceſs, as ſhe ſeems to be a deſerving little girl.

D 3

N. B.

N. B. We particularly recommend to her, that she would leave off the disagreeable frown which at times she wears, on her pretty face: it may be of service at particular periods, but must lose its effect with her swains, when made so free with.

Miss W-rd.   *In Rupert-street, opposite George-Court.*

" *So fond of the joy that flows from each kiss,*
" *She quits not her hold till doubled the bliss.*"

This girl has remarkable good eyes and fine teeth; but, in saying this, we say nothing in comparison to those hidden charms from whence the greatest raptures of love and enjoyment proceed. Think on the firm, globular, heaving breasts, that by the touch you are excited to make further advances to the termination of bliss, and in that itself the most perfect of her sex: so formed by nature, that the male can repeat enjoyment without quitting the premises—a perfection seldom to be met with among women of her occupation. She was debauched by an Oxonian, who soon after went into orders and forsook her, upon which she was determined to throw herself
felf

felf upon the town, and take her chance
like many more of her unfortunate fex.
She is extremely good-tempered, and
poffeffed of fuch a kind of pride, that
fhe would rather ftarve than return to her
friends.

Mrs. Pl--dw-ll. In the court behind Long-Acre Bagnio.

" *With majeftic air fhe charms Divines* "

Here lives a lady of a noble prefence,
great good-nature, with little or no affectation. Her beft friend is a Clergyman, who fpends his money very freely,
and devotes the beft part of his time to
her without excefs he enjoys the comely fair, and never intrudes when fhe is
diverting herfelf with her favourite; he
has his particular days for vifiting her,
often makes an excurfion with her into
the country, from whence he often returns without the leaft carnal knowledge
of her. He fixes fome particular days
for the improvement of her morals, and,
by dint of enforcing his gentle precepts,
he has made her as good a Chriftian as
any of her fphere.

Betfy

Betſy W-lſ-n. *At a Peruke-maker's, in*
Berwick-ſtreet.

" *No charms, with* Bet, *ſo much excel,*
" *As thoſe of brandy, hot as hell.*"

This girl is a brown, agreeable girl;
tolerable good legs, and always ready
for the ſport: ſhe has been kept for
ſome time by a tradeſman, by whom ſhe
has had two children, both now living.
Being rather fond of this man, ſhe is in-
tolerably mercenary: the money or preſent you are to give, engroſſes her whole
thoughts whilſt ſhe is in the very act.——
Brandy is what ſhe has the ſtrongeſt paſſion for. So callous are ſome of theſe
girls, that they would rather drink a
bumper of brandy or rum, than enjoy
the fineſt young fellow in the kingdom.

*M*rs. Pr--ch--d, *alias* Br--n. *Coal-ſhop,*
Wardour-ſtreet, Soho.

" *Oh ſhe does ſteel th' impriſon'd ſoul,*
" *And wrap it in Elyſium.*"

This lady is a native of Suſſex, from
whence ſhe was ſeduced by a ſon of
Mars, and coming up with him to London, reſigned the full poſſeſſion of her
charms.

charms. A few days, however, faw her at home again, but, inveigled by one of her own fex, (who betray more women than ours) fhe returned to London, and fortunately fell into very good hands, the gentleman from whom fhe takes her name, which is now about fix years fince. With him fhe lived till within thefe two years, and the fault why fhe did not remain with him longer feems to have been her own.

When fhe firft came to town, fhe was remarked for a handfome likenefs of Lady Sarah Bunbury, but, by a mifcarriage and a child, her face has rather loft its plumpnefs, and acquired a greater delicacy. She has fair hair, a good fkin, and pleafing features. The warmth of her bofom is a better recipe for impotency, than every ftimulus and provocative the whole materia medica can furnifh. She can wake to life the fleeting fluggifh fpirits, and give to age itfelf the vigor even of youth, and he, who rifes from her bed, finds himfelf only tired, not cloy'd or fatiated.

Mr. R⸺ha⸺dfe⸺n, a broker in the city, had an acquaintance for fome time with this lady. She complains of his ingratitude, how true we will not take upon

us

us to determine—perhaps, like Incle in the Spectator, he regretted his loft time, and endeavoured to make himfelf fome amends.

She is often in the two-fhilling gallery at Covent-Garden. Nanny, the orange woman, will direct any whom curiofity may prompt to enquire for her.

Mifs H-ſſ-y. *At Mrs. Giffard's, Mart-let-Court, Covent-Garden.*

" *Behold a ripe and melting maid,*
" *Bound 'prentice to the wanton trade.*"

This lady's features are very agreeable and tolerably regular, which, with a plump and pleafing figure, and lovely breafts, make her, though a woman, the father of luft, which fhe begetteth on every eye that fees her. She has brown hair, is young and of the middle fize, and when only *fome* of the fenfes are to be gratified, fhe cannot fail of pleafing.

Sometimes fhe takes a cup too much, and then woe be to them that fall under her difpleafure—all the mifchievous weapons fhe can lay her hand on are fure to be thrown at the culprits heads, and happy if they efcape unhurt !

Ye Gods ! what havock doth the---BOTTLE make
'Mongft woman-kind !

Mifs

Miss W-ll--gh-y, *alias* P-tr--ge. *Jelly-Shops.*

" *Does not always unsuccessful prove.*"

We are always happy to have an opportunity to praise distinguished merit. Beauty in a flattern will please but a short while, but neatness must be ever engaging, there is something so inviting in it, that, if its conquests are not so rapid, they are commonly more lasting.

If this lady has not been favored with extravagant gifts of beauty, she has an appearance that is very agreeable. She is rather short, with brown hair, about 25; and, as palates in no two men are alike, we doubt not but this lady has her share of favors.

We beg leave to recommend this piece of advice to the ladies, that a clean linen or stuff gown appears to more advantage, than a greasy trollop in filk, however rich it may be.

Miss Rebecca Sm—h. *Cumberland-Court.*

" *Oft she rejects, but never once offends* "

It may seem absurd to our readers to tell them, that a girl should refuse a good
offer,

offer, yet we can, of our knowledge, declare, Miſs Sm——h has refuſed a very good one from a perſon of Covent-Garden theatre, whether from *caprice, whim,* or, by keeping him a long time hungry, to make him pay a high price for his meat, or what other motive we are at a loſs to account. The greateſt generals ſometimes miſcarry, and poor Sm——h's ſchemes, if ſhe had any, came to nothing. for Reaſon aſſumed her throne, paſſion immediately decamped, and the youth was cooled without the aſſiſtance of her charms.

She has dark brown hair, wanton eyes, which ſhe well knows how to uſe, and, though fault may be found with many of her features, yet ſhe is upon the whole an agreeable woman, about 25, and has had the good luck to have been ſeveral times in keeping.

Miſs R-ſht-n. King-ſtreet, Soho.

" *'Tis eaſy to deſcend into the ſnare* "

Miſs R-ſht-n has a fine body for luſt, if it could be inſured from diſeaſe. Her ſkin is tolerable good, her eyes dark and piercing, hair deep brown, about 23, plump, and indeed a genteel faſhionable girl.

girl. Has a very good hand at getting into prison, having visited the inside of the Marshalsea twice within these last six months; however her creditors are not very obdurate, a few weeks confinement satisfies them, and Miss sallies forth to find fresh dupes, who are credulous enough to trust her.

This lady has chosen her favorite from among the musical tribe. Mr. B-k-r, who sung at Finch's Grotto-Gardens, fills her enraptured arms—when not better engaged.

Miss J-n-s. *At a Shoemaker's, in Tower-street, Seven-Dials.*

" *When foul disease attacks the frame,*
" *The lancet's mark becomes a shame.*"

A tall, genteel girl, very good-temper'd, and enjoys her bedfellow with the greatest extasy, but, having been too fond of the sport, and not cautious enough in her choice of lovers, she has unfortunately undergone the incisions of the groin, the marks of which she bears strongly, and in some measure anticipates the pleasure one would otherwise have with her She has a very good voice, and some notion of spouting, which

E

has

has given her a kind of paffion for the ftage, on which fhe is very defirous of going.

Mrs. R—g—rs.

" *Oh,* Polly! *you might have toy'd and kifs'd;*

" *By keeping men off, you keep them on.*"

This lady, who refides in Newcaftle-court, Butcher-Row, is ftill in her prime. She is about the middle fize, rather inclined to the *embonpoint.* She has good dark eyes, and black hair, a fine air, a handfome bofom, and is an excellent bed-fellow.

Maria derives her prefent name from a tradefman, with whom fhe lived, for fome time, upon fuch a footing, as to be efteemed his wife. She afterwards made a connexion with a furgeon, and this intimacy only fubfided with his life. The lofs of this laft admirer was a fevere ftroke upon her, as fhe not only loft her lover, but a confiderable fum of money, which fhe had lent him upon an emergency, and for which fhe had taken no fecurity.

Mrs R-g-rs has many amiable qualities fhe is naturally good-tempered, focial, and untinctured with the many little

arts

arts practised by that part of the sex, who give themselves up to promiscuous gratification. In a word, she is a good worthy sort of a woman, and deserves a better fate.

Mrs. J—ckf—n.

" *Some men to pleasure some to bus'ness take,*
" *But ev'ry woman is at heart a rake.*"

Mrs. J-ckf-n, who resides in Little Wild-street, Lincoln's-Inn-Fields, is the constant friend and intimate of the above lady, and carries her friendship so far as to have refused some good offers that have been made her by the known ac-quaintance of Mrs. R-g-rs.

Miss W—th—ft—ne, *alias* Pl--k-t-n.
Little Russel-street.

" *The careless fond unthinking mortal cheats.*"

This lady has a tall fine figure, fair hair, grey eyes, and an agreeable lisp in her speech. Her first name she bor-rowed from a lieutenant of the navy, with whom she was a long time. The latter name some say is really her own, having received it in marriage from a young fellow, who, doatingly fond of her, sacrificed every thing to his passion. Numberless are the misfortunes she has

drawn

drawn on him by her extravagance, and yet her ill treatment to him is almoſt beyond belief· but, ſpaniel-like, he kiſſes the hand that treats him ill. She has long been conſidered as a great addition to our liſt, being able to go through a great deal of buſineſs, and is an excellent friend to a tavern, as ſhe can carry off a great deal of liquor.

M.ſs Sm—thy. *Wardour-ſtreet, Soho, or Jelly-Shops.*

" *Do not venture where ſuch danger lyes.*"

Young, ſlim, and genteel, rather agreeable than handſome; fair hair, pock-marked, and about the middle ſize If a perpetual motion could be of ſerv ce, we would recommend this lady, as ſhe was never known to be a moment in one place—except in bed.

Mrs. J—m—s. *At Mrs. W—ll—ms's, Plough-Court, Fetter-lane*

" *A nothingneſs of ſoul and body.*"

This lady has nothing that we can perceive to recommend her to notice, unleſs being the occaſional companion, of the lady at whoſe houſe ſhe often is, and whoſe character may be found in this liſt. She fills up a gap, and, upon counting noſes,

nofes, might add to the number. We
wonder how fhe addreffed herfelf to us,
—but ftrange things do fometimes come
to pafs.

Mrs H—m—lt—n, *alias Lady* R—fe—ll.
New-Building, Oxford-Road.

" *A labyrinth where fools are loft.*"

This lady is the daughter of General
Pr—d—x, and born in wedlock. — Her
education was equal to her birth, but her
pride *even now* above it. She has lived
with feveral fince her elopement. Mr.
H—m—lt—n (known for diftinction by the
name of Splint) kept her a long while,
fince whom the public have enjoyed her.
Not long fince young Lord R—fe—ll, eldeft fon of the Earl of N—th—k, became enamoured of her, and the *kind*
creature followed him with his misfortunes to the King's-Bench, where he was
confined fometime for debt.

She is fhort, round faced, and plump;
her eyes fore and difguftful, her fkin,
indeed, good, but pock-marked ; her
hair blond, her countenance always
with a frown on—unlefs perhaps when
fhe puts on her holiday looks, which we,
who have known her a long time, never
remember her to have worn.

She

She ufed to be a great crony with Charlotte Sp—nc—r.

Mifs Tamer G—rd—n. *Near Long-Acre Bagnio.*

" *Her chains you'll find too difficult to bear.*"

Mifs G—rd—n is of Northumberland, which may be eafily diftinguifhed by her fpeech. Her mother and two other fifters came with her to London about a law-fuit, the fuccefs of which not anfwering their expectations, with fome other concurrent circumftances, drove her to us about five years ago.

She has a fine round face, pleafing figure, and limbs moulded like a Venus; affable, and extremely good-natured.— But here her qualifications ceafe, for in the rites of Venus fhe is as cold as a Dutch woman; from whence we naturally fuppofe the inconftancy of her lovers. Her other fifters are among the nymphs, but where we are totally ignorant.

We wifh fhe would not drink fo much, as nothing hurts both health and beauty like it.

Mifs Poll D—v—s. *At the Jelly-fhops.*

" *Subftantial happinefs* "

Is a tall, plump, genteel woman for her fize; brown hair, good eyes and
teeth;

teeth; walks well, and is about 28: has the knack of keeping her lovers, when those of superior beauty pine hopeless all alone. Her fort lyes in bed, where indeed she has great merit. We mention this circumstance, as appearances are often very deceitful; for even *we ourselves* have thought to have met a Juno, and, Ixion-like, have but embraced a cloud.

Mrs. Abington. Southampton-street, Covent-Garden.

" *Do not venture where such danger lyes,*
" *But shun the sight of her victorious eyes.*"

Of all vices we detest ingratitude, and we are afraid this lady would accuse us on that head, if we did not acknowledge the favors we have received from her in her single state. About 13 years ago, Miss B—rt—n did not keep her coach, but has often been glad to take her place even behind that of the celebrated Lucy Cooper, when coming from the hop at Mrs. P—k's in Aldersgate-street, where she was famous for singing a song, and beating time with her elbow, like Mr. Shuter in *Love for Love*, this expedient has got her many a shilling, which the company have club'd to reward her ingenuity.

Some

Some time after she appeared at Drury-lane, in the character of Miss Lucy, in *The Virgin Unmasked*. After this she married a trumpeter, whose name she now bears, went to Ireland, where she staid some time, and improved herself in the theatrical way; and coming over with her favorite swain*, engaged again at Drury-lane; where, by her excellence in her cast of parts, (Mrs. Clive having left the stage) she stands unrivalled.

Mr. Ab—gt—n, her husband, sold her to Mr. —— for 500l and entered into articles never to molest him in the possession of her. The gentleman's death (by which she expected great things) freed him from his bargain, but they do not live together. She keeps an elegant house, and Mr. J—ff—s—n is constantly with her. Her salary, though genteel, is not sufficient to maintain her table and manner of living, but her amour with Mr —— sufficiently makes up the deficiency. She is remarked in the company for her compassion and good-nature. Can any of our readers suppose, from so humane a disposition, that she would suffer any gentleman to die with despair for her?

---

* A performer at Drury-lane.

her? No· we can affure them to the
contrary; but then the approaches muſt
be made the proper way; fighs and oaths
and fuch like ſtuff alone will not do;
a little of them may be proper, and alfo
to convince her you *really* are a gentleman.

N. B. She meaſures gentility by the
weight of the purſe.

Miſs Fr—r, *A Stocking-ſhop in Long-Acre*
" *Brings ſuch a weak and feeble joy.*"

A decent little girl. Her family have
greatly affifted the nymphs of the grove.
The old folks let out lodgings to girls,
and the daughters waited on them. The
eldeft long fince entered the lifts for herfelf; the one of whom we write was a
long while nibbling at the bait before
ſhe was caught. Mrs Pr—ch—d, mentioned in this lift, uſed frequently to take
her with her to the play, where ſhe ferved in the quality of *toad-eater.* An
officer has taken her entirely to himſelf
(as he thinks) and treats her in fuch a
manner, as muſt make fuch a life (if it
is poffible) very agreeable. Some fay,
that Capt. N—the—t has married her;
but we will not have fo mean an opinion
of the Captain's underſtanding, as there

is

is nothing extraordinary in either her person or behaviour to make her so captivating. She is slim, dark brown hair, but a middling skin, which is also pock-marked, and about the common size.

Miss Jane Co—tev—le. *In Piccadilly, near Clarges-street.*

" *Oh! how the mighty are fallen!*"

The bow window, facing the Green Park, is certainly an agreeable situation, nay a very eligible one, for a woman of Miss Co—tev—le's profession : it has a fine command of the Park, and a lady appears to great advantage at a window, leaning negligently on an arm fine moulded, and white as mountain-snow.

The late D—e of D—s—t entertained this lady for his private amusement, and therefore chose her residence so nigh his own : during his life she lived nobly, and also supported her aged father in affluence, but, poor man! her supply failing by the D—e's death, the father could not expect what she had not, and is now in the King's-Bench.

Jenny makes a shift to live and drag through life, though her Strephon is abroad. Her person is genteel, her features agreeable, fair complexion, very

chatty,

chatty, good company, her height about the middle, and rather plump.

We condole with this lady on the lofs of her lord, and wifh her a change of circumftances, as nothing can fo much affect a woman of fpirit, as to be pitied.

Mifs ʃ—ckʃ—n. *At the Cat in the Strand.*
" *The rapture is not worth the pains it cofts.*"

This lady has lived fome time with farmer Ew—n, a man well known at the above houfe. She is looked upon as one of the fixtures of it, and, fhould the houfe be difpofed of, fhe would certainly go with the leafe.

She is tall and lufty, a little pock-marked, brown hair, dark eyes, walks well, and would be an agreeable woman, had fhe any converfation—but what fhe has.

'I will not, perhaps, be malapropos to mention the above houfe, and its œconomy. The mafter of it was a bailiff's follower, his wife his equal in every *po-lite* accomplifhment, and this agreeable jolly couple fatten upon the miferable gains of a few wretched women, to whom they will often lend five or ten guineas; but, in return, the poor girls are obliged to be there every and all the day, fpend-

ing

ing their money, or, the Marſhalſea's the word. To paint them in their true light, would almoſt exceed belief,—and we would not be ill-natured.

Mrs. F–ll–r, alias B–rr–tt. Mount-Row, Lambeth.

" *Conſider ſoberly of things.*"

Mrs. F–ll–r ſometime ſince lived in Mercers-ſtreet, where ſhe kept a houſe. Here ſhe was acquainted with that extraordinary genius Cary El—s, whoſe feats are too well known to need our repeating. Since that ſhe made a connexion with the very conſcientious Mr. Robert B–rr–tt, the auctioneer, and to whom ſhe ſays ſhe is married. She kept a houſe in partnerſhip with another lady in Northumberland-ſtreet. Since that ſhe has followed the fortunes of Mr. B–rr–tt, and even ſupplied him with caſh whilſt in the Fleet; and indeed has been as conſtant as the nature of her buſineſs would let her.

She is a fine tall luſty woman, fair ſkin, dark brown hair and eyes, walks well, but is very low bred; however ſhe has good-nature, and indeed appears (if ſhe has not ſenſe) to have a great deal of honeſty for the profeſſion.

Mrs.

Mrs. F—b—s. Back of Yeoman's Row, Brumpton.

" *'Tis now before you, and the pow'r to chuse.*"

Mrs. F—b—s takes her name from a General fo called, to whom fhe pretends fhe was married, but we give no more credit to this than we fhould to any part of her own ftory, had fhe the telling of it. She is about 36, very much pitted with the fmall-pox, light brown hair, rather above the common fize. How fuch a piece of goods firft came to our market we are at a lofs to guefs; we have indeed heard that fhe lived fome time fervant in Wapping, and, as the tars are good-natured, free-hearted fellows, and, after long voyages, are not very nice in their choice, they might perhaps have done her a *good-natured action*, this is the only way we can account for it, every other feems abfurd to us. Her hands and arms, her limbs indeed, in general, are more calculated for the milk-carrier, than the foft delights of love, however, if fhe finds herfelf but in fmall eftimation with our fex, fhe repays them the compliment, and frequently declares that a female bed-fellow can give more real joys than ever fhe experienced with the male part of the

F * * * *fex

fex: perhaps her demands in that way may be fo great fhe never found a man able to fupply her, this is but a natural conclufion, when a lady is remarked for paying vifits to a fellow famous only for ideotifm. The proverb indeed is on her fide, and perhaps fhe has found it true. The ingenious author of the Woman of Pleafure has given us a noble picture of it in the foolifh nofegay-man

Many of the pranks fhe has played with her own fex in bed (where fhe is as lafcivious as a goat) have come to our knowledge; but, from our regard to the delicacy of the fex, are fuppreffed, but in no fort as a favor to her, our plan indeed is too confined to admit of it · but we can affure her, unlefs fhe gives over that fcandalous itch of hers to fow diffentions where harmony and peace fhould ever reign, and which fhe envies becaufe fhe cannot attain to—we fhall not forget her next year, but be more explicit—and moreover acquaint her old drone of a keeper, in King's-bench Walks in the Temple, of her lewd pranks and amorous feats.

M.fs S—br—ght. *Haymarket, at a Barber's.*
" *She'd rather widen than clofe up the wound.*"

Lord G——lle was highly enamoured

moured of this lady, gave her all his Countess's clothes (at her decease), and many times has been seen with her in the stage-box, where a remarkable humor of his was to drink porter with her. They however quarrelled, madam pretended to be jealous, and carried the jest so far, that he swore the peace against her, and Sir John Fielding, for want of bail, committed her to Bridewell. Here finished her grand career afterwards she kept a house in Bow-street, but her good-nature undid her.

She is an excellent piece in bed, and is allowed on all hands to be a pretty woman, her face is plump and pleasing, her eyes good, fine dark brown hair, with an agreeable figure. Our readers will please to observe, we have not mentioned a word about her understanding; yet we are never more happy, than when we can with justice praise a lady's qualifications.

Mrs. Gr—es   Scotland-Yard.

" *You know the danger* "

This lady kept a house in Bow-street; but, business not succeeding, she was obliged to decamp, and take up her residence in the Verge. She was lately a prisoner in the King's-bench, and even

there

there she followed her business, and sold punch, though contrary to the established rules of all prisons.

She is a tall woman, tolerably well-made, little pock-marked, good eyes, but appears to be very haggard —all things decay. She has been at Portsmouth in the laudable calling of bum-boating, more politely stiled a green-grocer. In short, she will stick at nothing to get money, and that even by not the most honorable means.

We recommend honesty to this lady, as in the end she will find it the best policy.

Miss Gr—*a*—*se.* *Cumberland-Court, Drury-lane.*

——————————— *" She'll give*
" Whate'er you ask, nay all you can receive "

This lady having been distinguished by princely favor, we think she cannot fail of being an acceptable object to our readers.

She is the daughter to a servant at Mr. D—ffi—ld's, in Little - Chelsea, where she was brought up in the laundry, but ironing not agreeing with her inclination, and thinking herself male to move in a higher sphere of life, she quitted
ted

ted the ironing-board, and launched into life

Her firſt lodgings in the public way, was in Long-Acre, at a mantua-maker's, the corner of a court , here ſhe lodged ſometime, and ſeverely felt the effects of a certain diſorder. She removed from hence to a more commodious and elegant apartment, next the Coach and Horſes, in Great Marlborough-ſtreet, where ſhe lodged when ſhe came acquainted with Mrs. Mahon, for whoſe benefit at Co-vent-Garden theatre ſhe played the part of Polly in the Beggar's Opera, with ſome applauſe her affectation was no recommendation to her in it.

Soon after ſhe beheld the late D—ᵏᵉ of Yᵒᵣk, her admirer, and through whoſe intereſt with Sir Thomas Robinſon, ſhe was preferred to ſing at Ranelagh her voice indeed was no great recommendation, but her intereſt was ſufficient for one of leſs merit She performed there but one ſeaſon, and, at the death of his R—l H————ſs, left this kingdom for Ireland where ſhe now is, but ſhortly intends to viſit us She is rather tall, ſtrait and well-made, her hair rather approaching to red, her features ſmall but

F 3   pleaſing,

pleasing, her skin fair and soft, and at this time about 25.

We cannot think her any thing extra-ordinary, the close attachment of the D—e to her made her be much taken notice of, and served to heighten her vanity, which was a pity, as she had full sufficient long enough before· even in the laundry she was remarked for being haughty The old laundress always prophesied her pride would be her ruin, and how true her prediction!

Miss W—lf—n. *Northumberland - Court, Charing-Cross.*

" *At a distance charms our sight.*"

A fine mould to cast grenadiers in. She is not only tall, but her limbs are stout, and her body proportionably lusty. Her hair is a dark brown, her eyes the same colour, her features large, her skin rather brown.

She is the most indefatigable woman in the profession, and having no passions but for dress, she cares just as much for one man as another indeed, as is the fashion with all *fine* women, she does distinguish one as a favorite, as she hates to be out of the taste. She will walk

from

from Charing-Cross to the 'Change and back, to get a curse, (a whore's curse, we mean, 5s. 3d). She seldom turns away money, and is fond of old men; for, as she has no regard to what is called pleasure, and looks on it as a trouble, she likes them best, as they pay for what they cannot do. She is always well dressed, and very decent in her carriage and behaviour.

Sophia W—ft—n. *At Mrs P. B—rf—y's, Bow-street, Covent-Garden.*

" *Ignorance no longer can attone,*
" *When once the error and the fault is known.*"

Sophia has left her business of a milliner, to which she was 'prentice in the city, about four years, which time she has spent at Mrs. P. B—f—y's and Mrs, Fr--l—d's, the former of whom has been exceedingly kind to her in taking care of her, and preserving her clothes and neceffaries; for Sophy will dram it, and sometimes too much, and to get the dear creature, will part even with her shirt

Sophia is rather below the middle size, has dark brown hair, eyes of the same colour, and pretty good, her mouth not the best, the rest of her features really tolerable. She is far from being a beauty, ty, being too lusty for her height, but notwithstanding, a good-natured affable girl, and one that a man might take a night's lodging with without being disgusted in the morning, as every thing with her is natural—and never uses paint.

Miss Fl—m—g. *King-street, St. Ann's, Soho*

" *Fl——g has charms I own.*"

A tall and rather genteel woman, with fair hair and comely features, her skin good, but a little pock-marked.

She is commonly at home at her apartments, which are very genteel, neat, and rather elegant. She has a select set of friends, and therefore is seldom seen at any public place of resort without an acquaintance.

Her behaviour is very genteel when she has a mind, but she can upon occasion let fly a volley of small shot; but who, when they are provoked, have an absolute command of their tongue? We must always overlook small faults they who look for faultless pieces may save themselves the trouble of reading this book Her dress is always in taste, and indeed rather elegant than otherwise.

Miss

Mifs A——ms.   *At Mrs. Fr——l——d's, Bow-street, Covent-Garden.*

" *A filthy conqueft only you might boaft.*"

Come forward, thou dear, drowfy, gin-drinking, fnuff-taking Mifs A——ms: What in the name of wonder could influence you to leave a profeffion in which you was bred, for one to which you do not appear to have the leaft pretenfions. I muft own, I cannot fay what hidden charms you may poflefs. Don't you think thofe arms and hands of yours had better ftuck to their original calling, cleaning of grates, fcrubbing of floors, and keeping a houfe neat and clean, than drinking arrack - punch, getting drunk, and fetting up for a fine lady? But foft. we are finding fault with the wrong perfon; 'tis your admirers who are to blame, that are fo blind not to diftinguifh between the girl of beauty and merit, and a drunken fnuffy drab, who is generally to propofe a queftion or give an anfwer.

First, Major H——k——s, what crimes muft he have to anfwer for, in bringing you away? And then that old fool Mr. Wh——m——e, that idle C——mmiff——r of the St——mp-Office, how ftupid muft he be not to fee through your manner of living!

how

how choice is his taste to support, you —
However 'tis well for you, you have so
good a friend to your back — " Fools
have fortune, and knaves have luck."

Miss A—s is rather under the middle
size, fair hair, grey eyes, tolerable good
skin, pock-marked a little, and may easily be known by the quantity of Scotch
snuff she takes, particularly when she is in
liquor, when her upper lip is pretty well
covered with it, and does not badly re-
semble a pair of whiskers. Her breath,
from drinking, has acquired a very disagreeable smell how her friend recon-
ciles this, we cannot say, he must certainly have no nose —" A t—d's as good
for a sow as a pancake "

Miss R-shb—k. With Mr. M⸳B—n, in
the King's-Bench

Poor R-shb—k ! how thou art fallen,
from the gay, the lively, sprightly girl
—the toast of hundreds—the support of
Mrs Fr—l—d's—the delight of a host
of Quakers, to descend to take up with
a taylor, the ninth part of a man—a fellow made up of old measures and list—a
cabbager of cloth—a botcher. Oh, fye
for shame ! and thou to join him in the
horrid profession, to sit with him cross-
legged

legged on the board, feating of old bree-
ches, and elbowing of coats, 'tis true you
was always remarked for a *button-hole*. but
no one meant the making of it. Who
would have thought it? But love does
strange things—turns one topfy-turvy, as
for example—a very clear one indeed :
but, however, if Mifs R—fnb—k finds
content and happinefs in a prifon, 'tis
full as much as fhe could expect out of it ;
a prifon in this cafe is a palace Mifs
R—fhb—k indeed was once a prifoner
there againft her will, and, during her
abode there, was the lovely Sarah to two
brothers of the ftiff-rumpt fect, one of
whom now keeps a fhop in Newgate-
ftreet, and the other was excommunica-
ted by the brethren for his vices—running in debt without money to pay.

Mifs R—fhb—k is now too far advan-
ced, to think of fooling away her time ;
we doubt not but fhe has fome end in
what fhe is doing, I make no doubt but
fhe expects the taylor to marry her, and
fo give her a feat of work for life : indeed
it is high time for her to take up, fhe
has gone through a great deal of fervice,
and, as the corporal fays, " fire and
fmoke will tarnifh." She is now about
27, and one may fee that time has put

his

his claws upon her face, and, like the connoiſſeurs, put the ruſt of age upon a modern piece: her figure is about the common height, brown hair and eyes, ſkin middling, her features the ſame—very much changed from what we once knew her.

Mrs. D—bſ—n. Martlet-Court, Bow-ſtreet, Covent-Garden.

—————————— *" Her eyes impart*
" Delicious ruin and a pleaſing ſmart."

Alas, poor Doctor! how ſhe has anatomiſed thee.—Oh! fleſh, how thou art fiſhified—thou haſt no more roe than a ſhotten herring.

Mrs. D-bſ-n's charms are indeed powerful, but we could not have thought they would have wrought ſuch a powerful change in any man. The Doctor has been ſadly led by the noſe, but that is not his fault, it may more juſtly be laid to his ill-fated ſtars, for a man to make himſelf ſo truly ridiculous muſt certainly be under ſome planetary direction.

Mrs. D-bſ-n is about 30, rather luſty, good ſkin, dark brown hair, and tolerable features. What charms ſhe may have in celebrating the rites of Venus we cannot determine, but we entertain no

great

great opinion of her intellects, tho' she has cunning and art which may pass upon some as the same thing, 'tis not every one can distinguish the difference. answer Doctor if you don't think her the paragon of her sex? if you say no, your behaviour gives your tongue the lye.

Miss R-b—f-n.   At the Jelly-shops.

" *A_oid the danger which you ought to fear.*"

This lady is a jew but has no objection to a bit of christian flesh——but not in Shylock's way, she chufes her's lower, and lefs than a pound will satisfy her. She was a long time confin'd in the Marshalfea, and during the whole winter charitably supplied the prifon with *firing*: she is not long at liberty, and I suppose will confer the same favour on many a *poor* gentleman the approaching cold feafon: 'tis faid the Jews have no regard for the gentiles, is not this a convincing proof to the contrary? She was fo very good natured to Mr. Pillow, a young quaker, a fellow prifoner with her, that they fay she gave him fufficient to keep him *warm* for two or three years. She is rather tall, dark brown or rather black hair, large dark eyes and eye brows, a flim and genteel made girl——but rather too flat.   G   A f

Mifs H-ff-y. *No.* 12, *Dartmouth Row, Weftminfter.*

—————————" *Here poffefs*
" *Joy and fubftantial happinefs.*"

Mifs H-ff-y is really a very pretty girl, has very pleafing fparkling little eyes, tho' grey, her hair light brown, her fkin good, her features pretty regular, her lips agreeably pouting and a fine cheft.

She indeed has fome qualifications for her profeffion, and might ve think get money, but alas ' luck is all, 'tis in this as in all other bufinefs, the beft workmen are not always the richeft, however, we believe fhe makes a fhift to live and is always very genteel in her appearance, her manners correfpond with it, and her little chit chat is not unentertaining; one indeed of her front teeth is going to leave her mouth, having, for a long time paft, been thinking of it, and his next neighbour we believe muft follow him— this tho' we affure our readers is only thro' accident, we acquaint them of this left they fhould make illnatured conjectures—but fhould fhe lofe them both — fhe will be allowed pretty in fpite of her teeth.

Mifs

Mifs B-r-h.   *At a Chymift's in the Hay-market.*

" *Here with a little toil retreive your heart.*"

Mifs B-r-h lived not long fince in Princes-ftreet Drury-lane, and frequented the Jelly-fhops—then removed to Draper's Court, Lothbury. to live regular with a citizen, who commonly called on her before, or after change—and examined how *things ftood*. She is now for her infidelity to him returned to her old calling—Strange that woman cannot be content!—But tis 'in vain to advife; 'tis not fo much the lucre of gain as the name of *keeper*. Women cannot bear reftraint, and always think thofe pleafures fweeteft which they are moft ftrictly forbid to tafte. This was poor B-r-h's cafe, and fhe paid for her folly.

She is a pretty girl, about the middle fize or rather under it, plump, but not too fat; brown hair and eyes, good complexion, and well enough to pafs She is, however, a good bedfellow, and makes amends in bed for whatever qualifications fhe wants at the table.

Mifs

Miss S—th, *nicknamed* Blasted. *At the Jelly-shops.*

" *The very refuse of Mankind.*"

Some epithets are not very properly apply'd, or with justice, but we must allow the justice of this; if there could be one more infamous this lady is very deserving of it, she is the very Billingsgate of her sex; the whole society of fish women are mild, meek creatures, when put in competition with her · the back of the Point at Portsmouth she would even put out of countenance, and there is no withstanding her *oratory*, 'tis so very powerful.

S—th is rather under the middle size, fair hair and skin, grey eyes, and inclined to fat. We have lately seen her *padding* Fleet-street and its environs—suppose all her friends are tired of her company—however, if any of our readers should have the curiosity to hear this remarkable person, she is very easy to be found.

Mrs. M—ne. *At Newington Surry, or the Jelly-shops.*

" *A certain danger for a doubtful prize*"

A tall, bouncing wench with a crooked

ed nofe, brown hair, and middling features. When fhe was with Lieut.
M—ne, on board a floop of war at Ply-
mouth, fhe was a modeſt, decent woman, and could hardly fay bo to a
goofe, but that is ten years fince · fhe
now is very handy with a bottle, glafs,
or candleſtick to throw at your head, if
you fhould chance to affront her,—'tis
plain fhe has been in London all this
time for nothing.

Her art, in feducing the youthful part
of our fex, has brought no lefs than three
to the gallows that have come to our
knowledge, how many more fhe may
have fent that way we know not, but
we think we do not over-rate her abilities
at half a dozen—very agreeable reflec-
tions of a morning, if fhe has any feel-
ings, and has not parted with every
fpark of humanity !

Mifs T)----ll's   At the Haymarket
" *No ſtormy paſſions read in her breaſt.*"

A good-natured, eafy, foolifh girl,
about 19, brown hair, and middling
features; but we need not be particular
in our defcription of her, our readers
muſt have remarked her at Foote's, where
fhe played all laſt fummer. She left as
with

with her mother, and tho' she is at no expence for bed or board, yet, her salary is insufficient, and like the Welch parson —she is obliged to *do* a little to make it out. Her parts, indeed, are none of the brightest, but what signifies that · Venus is not the goddess of wisdom; she may have talents another way, and 'tis sufficient to do one thing well : As both her undertakings are new to her, we cannot help wishing her success, however/she may want a good tutor in the theatrical business, she cannot complain in the other part of her profession, whilst she has the acquaintance of several of the performers of the above theatre.

Miss H--ton.   At the Jelly-Shops
" *Gives up her province and will silent sit.'*

Rather taller than the common size, brown hair and eyes, neat limbs and a tolerable good skin, her features are none of the best, but, however, they are passable, she was not long ago in the Marshalsea from whence she is but lately emerged.

Miss Ur---art.   At the Jelly-Shops.
" *Too mean for scandal's tongue*"
This girl takes her name from a young
fellow

fellow, a merchant's clerk, in the city, who thro' her extravagance was brought to the gallows; we wonder at his facination as she is a wretched piece altogether, a nasty, disagreeable, snutfy, ill-made woman, without even one requisite or good quality; walks like a parrot, and talks with all the cant of a methodist preacher.

Miss Wi----son.   Coldbath-fields.

" *Avoid the cup, there's poison in the draught.*"

To pretend to give a description of this lady would be dictating to our readers, all of whom must have noticed her, if not at Drury-Lane theatre, where she danced some seasons, at least at Sadler's Wells, where her whole family have entertained the town for a long time. She now and then performs the character of Columbine, but is chiefly a dancer, in which we have seen many who have not excelled her · 'tis true, her bulk is rather a hindrance to her agility, which may in some measure excuse her not being able to get off the ground (as the dancers term it) but, however, she is very decent in what she performs.

We are sorry to find she still continues

to

to tipple fo much, we thought the connexion fhe was engaged in (a Harlequin
of Drury-Lane) would have reclaimed
her, but, alas! habits become fecond
nature, and we might almoft as foon
wafh a negro white, as conquer them
when of very long ftanding.

Mifs Poll K—n—dy. *Shooter's Hill and*
Great Ruffel-ftreet.

" *Can praife and admiration move.*"

This lady may be well confidered as
our modern Thais: fhe has, indeed, ti-
ken a long time to rife to her prefent independency, but fhe has at length gained her point, a circumftance that few
women pay any attention to the prefent moments, they philofophically think,
are only theirs, and therefore are refolved
to enjoy them—let to-morrow provide for
itfelf. This doctrine, during the fun-
fhine of affluence, may be very agreeable, but it is not always to be fine wea-
ther, and youth and beauty laft not for
ever, nay more, the power of pleafing:
when fortune puts a good thing in our
way, we ought to make the moft of it;
it is very eafy to out-live a man's liking,
—and then, if a neft-egg is not in ftore,
it goes very hard indeed.

Mifs.

Miss K—n—dy well confidered this, and, from the bounty of her gallants, has fecured a very fnug annuity, befides a number of very pretty things called diamonds, plate, &c. and yet fhe has not given up her bufinefs—fhe knows the town too well—fhe knows her independency fecures her from contempt, and infures her lovers hearts, for, foolifhly, they believe her choice of them was made by her regard, and this makes them very bountiful; when, poor creatures, if they knew her as well as we do, the fcene would be mightily changed before them. She never knew what love was—fhe has not a heart even fufceptible of that paffion—'tis wealth that poffeffes her inmoft foul—'tis that which fhe enjoys when fhe folds you in her arms—'tis then, in idea, fhe thinks fhe beholds a diamond ring, a necklace, aigrette, or fome other bauble, which your lavifh bounty has beftowed upon her ·——Yet for all this we cannot blame her, mankind is all a cheat—fhe often receives but from the thief: the Broker juft come from the Alley, who, with his bulls and bears, has deluded the unwary wretch, brings her his ill-got wealth —the lawyer, having robbed his client, buys with the pelf a lodging in the her arms·—the doctor too (for doctors sometimes pay) sinks in her snowy arms, and, in return for her well-feigned passion, gives her the produce of a load of poisonous medicines:—the church too—but they are sacred !————

She is certainly the greatest calculator among her sisterhood: if a day passes with a friend without advantage to her pocket, she is sure to be doubly diligent the next. A story will elucidate this more clearly: One evening, having invited Sh——r to supper, he pressed to stay all night; she complied, all in the way of business, and instead of costing her to the play, he gave her orders—one hand washes the other·—But, to proceed, in the morning a gentleman called, with whom she had made an appointment, but forgot· the maid knew her cues, and, coming into the bedchamber where they lay, told her mistress, aloud, that the mantua-maker was below with her new sack for Ranelagh, and that if she did not try it on, 'twould be impossible to get it done in time. Neddy was easily won to let her get up; and down stairs she went to her gallant, where, in the dining-room, on the sofa, she made up for the loss of her night with Sh——r, and then
returned

returned to him again, wifhing the mantua-maker at the devil, and the maid too,
for calling her from her dear Neddy.

She is, in perfon, a good fine woman;
rather too lufty and going down hill;
but that is no fault of hers, fhe endeavours
to prevent its appearance as much as
poffible; her hair brown, her teeth middling, her complexion tolerably well;
but what fignifies it to her? fhe has
made her market, and cares not what
we or any one elfe can fay, it has ferved
her turn.

*Mrs. El<u>i4ab</u>-b<u>eth</u> W-t—m-n. To be found
at the King's-Arms, Catherine-ftreet.*

" *A friend to propagation.*"

Mrs. W-t—m-n, tho' perhaps we call
her out of her name, Mrs. Jacobs, if fhe
chufes it, is a fhort lady, fair complexion,
rather inclined to be lufty, and every
year obliges the world with a new mem-
ber: fhe is a fpirited woman, and will
not give up an inch of her prerogative,
ſomefaygoesbeyond it, but if we fuppofe
that, we muft pay a bad compliment to
Mr. J<u>aco</u>-bs, (a limb of the law) and that
would be fcandalum magnatum. Mr.
J—bs is famous for his great knowledge
of the common law, but, if he has half

as

as much in his head, as she has had in her *tail*, he is fit to be chief justice of either the King's-Bench, or Common-Pleas.

A haberdasher in Tavistock-street was a competitor for this lady, but law's *pen* and *ink* was too powerful for the haberdasher's *yard*.

Mrs. Th——nt——n *Facing the Bun-shop, near the Asylum, Lambeth.*

" *Ugly almost as sin.* "

We wonder what could induce this lady to take up a profession for the which she is no more calculated than we are to be archbishop of Canterbury, unless the success her sister has met with, whom we have mentioned under the name of Ed-m——ds Perhaps, influenced by that, she might hope success, but very vainly indeed, we must therefore conclude her glasses have the art to pay compliments. This must certainly have been the case; for no man could have told her so bare-faced a lye, as that she was pretty—unless in the dark ——To give a description of her would be paying her too great a compliment, as it would be impossible to be equal to the task The only situation in life we can recommend to her would

would be that of a toad-eater to fome lady, though indeed fhe is fo great' a flattern, fhe is almoft unfit for that, unlefs fhe alters from her prefent manner of dreffing.

Mifs Kitty H—rr—s   At the Cat in the Strand.

" *Severely rails at all fhe difapproves.*"

Kitty has a long time figured upon, and bandied about from one to the other She lived fome time at Hampftead, had an acquaintance with Capt. Uft—ke, and now lately was with a city attorney, Mr. Le Br—n. Sometime fince in a fray with Capt. N—g—t, fhe received a cut acrofs her wrift, the fatal marks of which remain, and ever will. She is a pretty blue-eyed girl, fair hair, good fkin, and rather under the middle fize, and plump. She is eternally at the Cat in the Strand, and one of its beft dupes, of which the miftrefs could fpeak the *truth*, but that's a commodity fhe has no dealing in, any more than honefty.

Mifs Cl—l—d.   At the Barber's, Newport-ftreet, Leicefter-Fields.

Mifs Cl—l—d takes her name from a captain in the navy, who, at the beginning

H

ginning of the peace was employed as ambaffador to the Emperor of Morocco; and was once highly enamoured of this lady.

She is a good fine figure, brown complexion, her hair of the fame colour, and knows very well how to behave · her paffions indeed are not very great, fo that fhe is rather better at table than in bed — excellence in every particular belongs to no woman. She has two fifters, who are alfo engaged in the fame laudable purfuits, and are known by the names of D⸺gl⸺y and So⸺rf⸺t.

She takes fometimes a cup too much, but is not very noify, or any ways troublefome, only joyous and frolickfome.

Mifs Pat L⸺e. *Martlet-Court, Bow-ftreet.*
" *Many accomplifhments in* Patty *meet.*"

This lady's principle of honefty has been remarked by all the fifterhood. She once figured on the ftage, ran in debt, and quitted this country for Jamaica, from whence fhe is not long returned, and has difcharged her debts with the greateft honour, tho' fhe might have compounded them for lefs than half their amount—an inftance not very common in greater pretenders to honefty.

She

She is said to be related to the D—wf—n family, whom we have mentioned in the characters *N—wt—n* and *Gr—ft—n.*

We are happy to have it in our power to praise the ladies, but most particularly in points of this kind · in addition to this valuable character, Miss L—e must be considered as a fine girl, rather taller than the common size, plump, and tolerable good features.

Mrs. F—wl—r. To be-found at C—rt—r's Bagnio, Bow-street

" *A Gorgon face, and serpent tongue.*"

This lady excels any we have mentioned—in ugliness. Her person coarse, her features the same, pock-marked, rude and uncouth in her behaviour; her skin we cannot say any thing about, as we are no judge of painting; and, notwithstanding, she is always well dressed: she married the son of a butcher in Bedford-street, whom she inveigled, and would have sent to the gallows, but, to his parents comfort, his death saved them much sorrow.

She possesses every thing, in our opinion, that is disgustful, drinks, takes snuff, and swears like a trooper. She kept not long since a bawdy-house, and

H 2   from

from that laudable profeſſion turned out again. She is about 36, and the ſooner we put an end to her character the better, as it is diſagreeable to write, and we are ſure muſt be ſo to read any more about her.

Miſs Kitty E---ſon.   In the King's Bench.
" *Kitty's not fair ; yet, Kitty's young.*"

This lady about four or five years ago was indeed a pretty girl, at that time ſhe was not ſuch a reprobate as at preſent, but, experience in all buſineſſes makes perfect. She can now toſs off a glaſs of gin as well as the commoneſt hunter in the Strand, and, like them, ſtoop to every meanneſs; yet, notwithſtanding, prides herſelf upon her character. She has been near a twelvemonth with a Mr Callender, and followed him with his misfortunes to the Bench, and endeavours to return the favours ſhe has received at his hands.

She is of ſhort ſtature, rather brown complexion, features rather maſculine for her ſize, and, indeed, has ſuffered much, (if, as is reported, ſhe was once pretty) but all things wear out Brooms will wear to the ſtumps. Seven years in conſtant uſe is a long time.

Miſs

Miss Alb—*tini. In Crown Court, Russel Street.*

" *Puts off impertinence for wit.*"

Miss Alb—tini, alias Dutchy, alias Jones, which last name most properly belongs to her, as she purchased it to secure her from her debts. She married Mr. Jones, who exercised the calling of a—link-boy, and for three guineas consented to be her spouse.

This lady's ingratitude is famous beyond every other part of her character. Poor Hudson, an officer in the East-India Company's service, after having spent several hundreds on her, was suffered, even when he visited her, to go in fear of the bailiffs for so trifling a debt as forty shillings, how she can reconcile this behaviour to his generosity and her affluence at the same time we know not, but it was to the last degree cruel. Kempson succeeded him , equally lavish of his bounty, and was soon obliged to embark for the East-Indies to repair his fortune, which her extravagance had almost ruined. These two gentlemen agreed very well together in the possession of her, being constantly there at the same time , but, it was plain, she gave

the

the preference to Kempſon, and for a good reaſon——he was then the richeſt. She is not the woman we ſhould chuſe: there is ſomething ſo forbidding in her countenance, tho' her features are pretty regular, her hair a gloſſy jet, her ſhape and carriage rather genteel. She is Dutch by birth; ſpeaks Engliſh rather broken, and is a daughter of ſome of the tribes of Iſrael.

Miſs Pat—ſon. *At a Hair Dreſſer's in Hart Street.*

" *Here tributary fops appear.*"

A fine, bouncing, crummy wench, taller than the ordinary ſize, fair hair, good ſkin, and pretty regular features, her converſation not very elevated, but great beyond conception, in the ritual way. An Upholſterer (a quaker) had the *ſpirit* to keep her ſome time, which did not coſt him a little, for ſhe is fond of dreſs and pleaſure, but ſhe has done his buſineſs, and, Obadiah, inſtead of every day in the week, only calls on ſundays. Her laſt keeper ſhe loſt by being too avaricious: he had agreed to pay ſome money for what ſhe had been arreſted, and, to add to the ſum, got herſelf arreſted again; but he ſaw thro' the cheat

and

and left madam in the lurch, to confole herfelf for the lofs of a good friend, by her being too much in a hurry to grow rich—a caution to the reft of the fifter-hood.

Mrs. Sturgefs.   In Cumberland Court, Drury Lane.

" *No ftormy paffions revels in her breaft,*
" *But all within is love, and peace, and reft.*"

Mrs. St———efs may be confidered as a very fine woman, having a good fkin, lively eyes and nofe, brown hair, and teeth no ways bad : her height is rather above the common ordinary fize, and fhe is agreeably plump and lufty.

She is the daughter of a Cheefemonger in Piccadilly, near St. James's Street, and has left home about eight or nine years. Laft War fhe made a campaign with an officer in Germany She has (however handfome) had fome fevere ftrokes of fortune, not always having been fo well off as at prefent. She has a houfe of her own elegantly furnifhed, and is in very good keeping ; but Poll Jump (for that is her proper name) is a true woman, fhe will ftand the touch when properly applied, as fhe is of opinion if ready at her keeper's call 'tis as much as

he

he can expect. No wonder infidelity
fhould be common with women of her
caft, when even the marriage knot cannot fecure mens *property.*

*Mrs. Cox—dge.   In Catherine Street, in the
Strand.*

" *A prieftefs of the Cyprian Deity.*"

She has contributed fo largely to oblige the public, both before fhe became
a prieftefs and fince, that it would be
doing her injuftice not to take notice of
her. Her endeavours have been crowned
with fuccefs, and fhe can fit down con-
tentedly, having amaffed fome money
to make her eafy. Her character too,
as a *houfekeeper,* has been always decent,
and fhe has had the addrefs to prevent
—" any knock-me-down doings in her
houfe," and, 'tis faid, notwithftanding
fhe has been a long time in bufinefs, and
not long fince lived within a door or two
of Sir John, fhe has not paid the juftice
above four or five vifits. Any Gentleman having a mind to try a fall with her,
(which, if he will pay a proper price, he
may do) the following is her defcription
fhort and fat, tho' not too fhort for her
bulk, good fkin, and fomething agreeable in her countenance; the fat has fo

over-run

over-run her face that it is almoft impoffible to have a peep at her features, and about 33 or 34. When fhe caters for herfelf (for fhe likes a little bit now and then) they fay fhe never goes out of *England.*

Mrs. Har——ton   Haddock's Bagnio,
Charing-Crofs.

" *The Goddefs of the place.*"

This lady has made herfelf pretty remarkable by her law-fuit with Mr. Hitchcock, in the Court of King's Bench, for the recovery of a debt, which fhe pretended was due to her, of 300l, fourfcore of which was for jellies; but the evidences fo confounded each other, that without examining any body on the fide of the defendant, a verdict was given in his favour, and fome of her *honeft* witneffes are likely to ftand in the pillory for perjury.

'T is furprifing that the younger ladies fhould be fuch dupes as to be mere jackalls to thefe very *honeft* old ones,—as to facrificing body and foul to their emolument alone, fcarcely getting food and raiment for all their trouble: by the honeft induftry of fome of whom fhe has amaffed fufficient to purchafe an eftate in the country,

country, where 'tis faid fhe intends to retire and live in folitude, and make up her accounts with heaven. We wifh fhe would fet about it fpeedily, as fhe muft have a very large bill to look over, little to ballance againft it, and unlefs fhe makes hafte, and alfo lives a long while, we are afraid fhe will not be able to difcharge it before fhe dies.

Nancy St———y. *Late of Portland-Row, No.* 59, *now in Scotland Yard.*

" *Deftructive love has been her bane.*"

This young lady is about twenty-four years of age, a very amiable figure, with good eyes, fine teeth, and incomparable good hair. She has had many opportunities of being provided for, in a genteel manner, but her paffions have ever been a bar to her intereft: fhe has been known to quit the rich citizen to fly into the arms of her favourite; and lately a very handfome Hibernian has folely engroffed her attention, without the leaft view of lucre. She is extremely good-natured, full of fpirits, and very obliging. What money fhe gets in the proftitutive way, is folely againft the grain. She feldom is prefented with lefs than two guineas, and that fhe thinks little about, as fhe is

much

much in debt, and indeed deserves a better fate.

Miss F—g—f—n. *In Rathbone - Place, No. 22.*

" *Her jetty locks my bosom fires,*
" *And kindles all my fierce desires.*"

A fine tall girl, black hair, good teeth; in reality, what may be called a very fine woman. She was debauched by L—d G—— about three years ago, has ever since rolled in a higher sphere than most in her way. Her price is five pieces, and seldom abates, unless she is fond of her gallant, or chuses to bestow her favours gratis.

Polly J—k—f—n. *Late of the above place, and now in Scotland Yard, with* Nancy St——y.

" *Youth without beauty has still its charms.*"

Polly is a little fluttering child, about fourteen years of age, has full dark eyes, and a projecting mouth, with tolerable good teeth; but upon the whole, nothing striking or extraordinary. If her youth, and her not being fledged, are recommendations, she is certainly possessed of them. She was debauched about ten months ago by the noted Capt. Jones, who

who was convicted of an unnatural crime: it feems to coincide with his love of fmall commodities, for to be fure Polly could not have been fit, at that time, for any man even of *middling parts*. She has paffed for a maidenhead fince that period twenty times, and is paid accordingly; and being under the direction of a very good lady, who directs her to play her part to admiration, fhe is in a fair way of getting money.

Mifs L⁴e. Glafs fhop, St. James's-ftreet.
" *Doats upon the filliest things.*"

This lady had a connexion with a co-median of Drury-lane, which has lately been broke off, for what caufe we can-not fay, and madam now depends upon the generous public for fupport, but fhe is not unacquainted with the bufinefs, fhe is only returned to her old calling. She is a pretty black girl, about the middle fize, with remarkable fine dark eyes and hair. Her fkin is very good, a little pock-marked, and not a bad companion.

She has performed two or three little characters at Foote's, and came off de-cently, and 'tis faid fhe intends to take up with the ftage, and live *honeft* —Very honeftly intended, but we are afraid it

is not a school to caufe fuch a happy reformation.

*Mifs C–pel—d. Portland-ftreet, St. Mary
le-bone, Perfume-fhop, No. 2 9.*   -
  " *Avaunt, thou race of Hibern'a !*
  " *Nor dare t'approach her charms.*"

This lady is a genteel, well-made girl;
brown complexion, good hair, and about
21 years of age , carries on a tolerable
bufinefs in the fornicative way , was a
particular favourite of Hoare, the Irifh-
man, who was tranfported fome time
fince. She has had feveral good offers
from Hibernians , but fince her connection with the above *gentleman,* has con-
ceived an antipathy to the whole country,
and rather take up with *fmaller matters*
from her own countrymen.

Mifs Pr—ce.

" *Truft not your eyes, for they'll your peace
betray.*"

This lady, who lately refided in Stone-
cutter Street, Fleet Market, a nd is now
taken into keeping by a rich Jew ; tho'
fhort, is above the common rank of Cyprian Devotees. Her features are un-
commonly regular, her eyes amorous
and expreffive, her lips pouting, her

I   teeth

teeth white and even, her bosom very inviting, and the lower part of her person is extremely seducing, she is besides, very good natured and convivial. She is not now twenty. Pr--ce is a miniature beauty, and, when she moves in a higher sphere, will certainly be a first rate toast We have the pleasure to hear she is in treaty with a man of great fortune.—We greet thee well, for thou art deserving of it!

Mrs. Fo––er. *Rosoman's Row.*

" *Gallants, beware, look sharp, take care,*
" *The blind eat many a fly* "

This lady whose genteel behaviour, animated with no small degree of vanity, might persuade one, from her first appearance, that she is a modest woman, is, nevertheless, among the number of come-at-able demireps, who meet you in a tete-a-tete, about three quarters of the way, to prevent mistakes from external prudery She, is it must be acknowledged a pretty little woman, has good eyes, and fine air, a handsome hand and arm, and a great deal of that small talk which women of this cast are so apt to take to pleasantry and wit. Her apparent disinterestedness is very seducing,

as

as she puts on all the airs of a woman of consequence, whose sole view in an intrigue is *pleasure*, but beneath this illusion, self-interest may easily be discriminated. She is, indeed, at that time of life when prudence ought to predominate over every passion, for she is about to and that period of life the most, and secure the greatest intelligence. Publications, &c. when you can't read, in the middle ages, behold a complete room to spare. When a woman perceives her beauty is decay, and finds every day estranges her still farther from her juvenile beauty, she regrets (if an amorous woman) the loss of every moment of her life that has not been consecrated to bliss, and risques an adventure that she would formerly have spurned, rather than lose the chance of an admirer, the perspective of a moment's enjoyment-

Mrs. Sa—ders. *In St Martin's Lane, opposite Beuer's Repository.*

"*Under how hard a fate are women born,*
"*Prais'd to their ruin or expos'd to scorn!*
"*If they want beauty they of love despair,*
"*And are besieg'd like frontier towns of war.*

This lady was, a few years since, a

       nursery

nurfery maid to a gentleman's family, in Brook Street, Holborn in which capacity fhe ufed frequently to walk for the air, with her little ward, in Gray's-Inn Gardens. A certain gentleman, of Coney Court, perceiving a very fine girl, which fhe was at that time, often in the walks, took an opportunity of converfing with her, and foon after perfuaded her to come and make fome tea for him in his chambers. The fequel. it were needlefs to relate. fhe was debauched, and foon after deferted by her betrayer The confequence of which, was having loft her place, and being deftitute of a chaicter, fhe was obliged to have recourfe to her beauty for a fubfiftance. She took lodgings in ―――― Street, Red Lyon Square, and had a number of fucceffive admirers She was, at this time, not above twenty, tall and well made, with a fine open expreffive countenance, large amorous eyes, her other features in due fymetr, her mouth very agreeable, and her teeth regular, in a word, fhe was at that time (about three years fince) one of the fineft women upon the town, and, accordingly, made one of the beft figures from the emoluments of her employment. She was fome time

after

after taken into keeping by a man of fortune, with whom she made a summer excursion into the country, but, upon his demise, her finances being exhausted, she was compelled to have recourse to a more general commerce, in which she has not been so successful as before, and chagrine added to the usual irregularities accidental to her profession, has diminished those charms which were before so attracting, her face is now rather bloated, and she is grown somewhat masculine in her person, she may, nevertheless. still be pronounced a very good piece, and a desirable woman.

Miss Mi—ell.

" *About your eyes the loves might ever play* "

This lady resides in Crown Court, Bow Street. She is not tall, but elegantly made, a fine bosom, regular features. most enticing eyes, an aquiline nose, the sure index of an amorous disposition in women; her complexion we cannot at present much recommend, but it is believed, that if her plan of life was more regular. certain little eruptions, which are now a foe to it, might certain-

ly

ly difappear, and then Mi—ell would be a charming girl indeed.

Mifs Ad—s. *New Buildings, Mary-le-bone.*

" *Oh! that a form fo lovely fhould e'er be frail* "

This lady is really fuperior to the ufual run of *come-at-able* women, her form is not only very enchanting, her countenance bewitching, and her very ringlets the *toils* of love, but even her underftanding has a bent of a kind very different from proftitution. This lady lives in a moft elegant manner, in Newman Street, Oxford Road: fhe has, neverthelefs, lately met with fome difagreeable fhades in the canvafs of her life, that have thrown a gloom over the whole portrait. We hope, however, that fhe will be able foon to difpel it, and *fhine* in a *vortex* fuited to her magnitude,

Mifs St—t—n.

" *'Tis true, 'tis pity*—*Pity 'tis t'is true!* "

Poor little St—t—n! unhappy even in your vices——Oh! that the wretch had ne'er exifted who brought you firft to this!

A jeweller, with whom fhe was ena-
morred

moured, feduced her to a lodging near the Vine tavern, Holborn. Here they for fome time paffed for man and wife: but, by his indolence, and her credulity, they were obliged to decamp at midnight. She has fince taken a lodging in Red-lion-ftreet, Holborn, and been obliged to fubmit to the precarious fupport of various lovers St—t—n was a very pretty little girl, finely formed, with an agreeable countenance, expreffive dark eyes, good teeth, and a clear complexion. She is now, indeed, much altered, but a little good living would bring her about, and fhe really deferves fattening.

Mrs Qu—l—i.

" *The fpecious matron, or the wanton wife!* "

This lady refides in Little Titchfield-ftreet, Cavendifh-fquare. She is a treffy figure, though not handfome, is a very convenient good-natured woman, and has officiated in the double capacity of miftrefs and procurefs. If you do not like her, fhe has generally a tolerable good piece in the firft floor, whom fhe recommends *upon honour*. At prefent her lodgings are empty, but fhe foon expects an agreeable lodger, as fhe has entered upon a new profeffion —a MIDWIFE. By
th.s

this means she has given sanction to a re-
treat to a woman of a tender character,
and either a *male* or *female* may lie in
there *very privately*.

Miss W—lk—s.

"*What an angelic face !—but what a form !*"

This lady very lately resided in Princes-
street, Bloomsbury, at a midwife's. She
is not above twenty, and has a very engaging countenance, with fine, dark,
melting eyes, and very regular teeth.
Her person does not entirely correspond;
she is short and very crooked, but she
has a certain latent charm that more than
compensates for any deformity of body.
In a word, take her all in all, she is a
very good piece, and, if you can forget
she is *hunch-backed,* she is a *little Venus.*

Miss M—lls.

" *I know the world, I know the world, &c.*"

This lady is under the middle size, a
pretty little girl, very good-natured, and
very accessible. She resides in Wells-
street, Oxford-Road, and has lately made
her appearance at the theatre in the Hay-
market, in the character of Ursula in the
Padlock.

Poll

Poll K—nn—dy. *Piercy-street.*

" *While in the circle of her arms I lay,*
" *Whole summers funs roll'd unperceiv'd away*"

This is a fine, tall, genteel girl, with amorous eyes, and pouting lips, who has taken upon herfelf the name of K—nn—dy, thinking there is fome charm in the found, and that, like the other Mifs K—nn—dy, in keeping by L— R——t Sp————r, fhe will make her way upon the *bon ton*, and be equally capable of ferving her relations upon every emergent occafion.

Mrs. D—f—r, *alias Mifs* R—ch—ds.
Near Taviftock Chapel, Bloomfbury.

" *Love, love, it is like a loofenefs,*
" *It won't let a poor man go about his bus'nefs.*"

This lady is now turned of 30, but is one of thofe pieces that wear fo well, fhe may with juftice be preferred to many under 20. She is rather below the middle fize, has good black eyes, and hair of the fame colour. She has a fine, clear, fmooth fkin, and her latent charms, it is faid, deferve peculiar praife. She has been in high keeping at different times, and may probably again flourifh in a

more

more elevated fphere, than that fhe at
prefent moves in, though her appearance
is always genteel, if not elegant. She
is a very conftant cuftomer to the firft
gallery, at half price, at either houfe,
and may generally be met with, at one ·
or other, on the right hand fide.

Mifs Fl—m—g. *Berner-ftreet.*
" *They fay fhe's* FAIR,—*I'm fure fhe's very*
DEAR."

An elegant girl, above the middle
fize, very fair, and very handfome.
This lady is defcended from a noble
Scotch family, and piques herfelf a good
deal upon her anceftry, but more upon
her beauty, and will not therefore grant
a *flying favour* under two pounds two.
However, many of her admirers think
fhe is worth the money.

Mifs. W—fe. *Prince's-ftreet, Leicefter-
Field.*

" *Limbs, do your office. Tear me to her,*
" *Then fail me if you can!*"

Mifs W—fe is a fine, tall, fhewy woman, though her portrait would not dif-
play the moft regular arrangement of
features, her face is very far from being
difagreeable. She refided for fome time
at

at the houfe in Leicefter-fields, where the unfortunate Mrs. K—g loft her life; but it feems, the effects of the remembrance of the fhocking fcene, that was tranfacted there, induced her to quit that place. This lady is now about fix and twenty, and we confider her as a valuable acquifition to our lift.

Mifs B—k—r.

" *Lovers hearts are not their own hearts,*
" *Nor lungs nor lights, and fo forth downwards.*

This lady, who refides in Caftle-court, Chandos-ftreet, feems to have confidered thefe lines of Hudibras literally and to have acted entirely upon this principle. She is neverthelefs a fine tall girl, not much above twenty, with expreffive blue eyes, a fair complexion, and light hair. But fhe finds her advantage in an entire condefcenfion to her admirers, as many perfons from the Eaft of Temple-Bar, who pay their weekly devotions at her fhrine, are as capricious in their defires as a fine lady in a toy-fhop, yet fhe adminifters to them every whimfical gratification for which he fails not to obtain a *proportionate* recompence

Mifs

Miss Kitty To–ll–r.   *At Mrs. E——ts,*
in George Street New Buildings.

" *Delicate her taste, and elegant her air* "

This young lady is one of the most delicate in her way, is extremely pretty, good hair, teeth, and fine eyes, she does not give her company to any body but those she is recommended to, and then the treatment she meets is always genteel. From two pieces to five is her price.

Miss Sally El—r.   *Wardour Street,*
opposite the Horse-shoe, Soho.

" *No face more fair, nor breath so sweet!*
" *Beauty's display'd from head to feet* "

Here you may with pleasure view one of the finest skins that ever was seen, her hair and teeth are wonderfully fine, with tolerable good eyes: Sally is also very well made, and is very fond of a bedfellow. She is a native of Ireland, and, like many of that country, can scarce refuse a pretty fellow any reasonable request, she is contented with little, and puts no price upon any body's pocket.

Charlotte

Charlotte Cum——ns. *Saffron Hill, near Hatton Garden."*

" *Hard is the fate of poor Charlotte."*

This poor girl, who really is very a-greeable, and rather of a modeft caft, never knew either father or mother, fhe was dropt by the latter when fhe was fcarce a month old, and being reared by an old woman, who fold falop, and who by accident found her at the ftep of a door in Holborn, was brought up to the age of 15, making her follow this poor bufinefs, when, upon the death of this woman, fhe thought proper to take to the bufinefs fhe now follows: fhe is very thankful for a quarter guinea, and feldom expects more.

Betfy Ha—ley. *At a Chandler's Shop, near Holborn Bars.*

" *Tho' deformed fhe ftill can pleafe* "

This is a little crooked girl, with good eyes and teeth, and a tolerable pair of legs; her hair is almoft entirely falfe; but fhe has the faculty of pleafing with her tail, and is always ready to oblige and turn her hand to any thing.

K   Polly

Polly Ham—ton. *In Union Street, near Well Street New Buildings.*

" *Engaging are the ways of pretty Poll.*"

A very agreeable piece, fair hair, and open countenance, tolerably well made, and rather upon the haut-ton. often sent for to houses in the private way, where she often gets two pieces, upon the whole, she carries on a good trade, and is likely to turn out a very prudent girl.

Miss Ver—n. *Frith Street, Soho.*

" *Her voice is love's alarm.*"

This lady is really a good figure, fine black eyes and hair, she passes to be pretty constant to a certain colonel, but by the quantity of diet-drink, which she drinks for a mistaken disorder, which she calls the scurvy, somewhat proves her to have been rather inconstant, and has suffered for it. She is very come-at-able—but never receives any company at her lodgings excepting the above gentleman. Two guineas is about her mark, and she will sing you an agreeable song into the bargain.

Polly

Polly Sp—ks. *At the Denmark Coffee House.*

"*Good nature and simplicity will ever bear the sway.*"

A main supporter of the above coffee-house. A pretty little girl, blue eyes, chatty and good-natured, nothing amiss in her person, except a little under size. She will drink a bottle of Madeira, partly because she is fond of it, and partly for the good of the house, after which she is ready for the highest bidder; in short, what by flyers and night works, she picks up a little money, and, upon the whole, is really a fit subject for a house of this kind.

Mrs. Li—ns. *In little Windmill Street, near Brewer Street.*

"*Chip in porrage, or a useful necessary.*"

Here you will find a plain girl, without much meaning, but tolerably good-natured; she is very clean between the legs, and, tho' rather wide, has the art of contraction, which is very useful to women of her profession; a quarter of a guinea is reckoned genteel, after which, either call or send, you are always welcome.

Miss

Miſs St. Cl—e. *Carrington-ſtreet, May-Fair.*

" *Her ſteps are by prudence guided.*"

If the loves and graces united can entitle a female to a rank among the firſt-rate meretricious toaſts, we think this lady can claim pre-eminence to moſt upon our liſt. She is at once beautiful and elegant, lively and agreeable. She cannot indeed claim the chaſtity of Diana, but ſhe can urge her plea to the art of pleaſing beyond a Thais. After ſaying this, it will be paying her no compliment to add, that the nobleman, who avows himſelf her protector, does himſelf honor in being her patron.

Miſs Gr——re. *No.* 5, *Chapel-ſtreet, Scho.*

" *From bad example we are led to vice.*'

This lady is a very agreeable, delicate piece, about 17. She has infinite good-nature, and actually ſupports her mother and ſiſter. Her particular friend is Sir W — P——, who imagines he has her entirely to himſelf, but we can aſſure our readers that ſhe is very comeatable, her price being about two pounds two. We may ſoon expect her ſiſter to enter

our

our lift, as she is always with her, and, no doubt, from the tuition of the one, the other muft foon inevitably learn her trade.

Mifs H—rt. *At the Coal-fhed, Wardour-fireet.*

" *Youthful and gay, fhe never fails to pleafe.*"

A pretty, delicate, young girl, who has been debauched but a few months, has the appearance of a girl of fome fafhion, and is really worth notice. She is incomparably well made, and has little or no affectation. For your two pounds two, you may enjoy here a very fnug piece, and through a little ftrength of imagination confider her as a maidenhead.

Nancy St—v—ns. *In a court near Temple-Bar.*

" *To refufe a man fhe holds a crime* "

This lady, who is really the daughter of a certain houfe-keeper, has been thro' a number of misfortunes, thro' her indifcretion. She was debauched by the Hon. M. N—, by whom fhe had a child She has fince been married, and chiefly given up a bufinefs, which fhe uled to follow, for fome time, however, fhe is, upon

proper

proper notice, to be had, and her price is reasonable.

Betsey B—l—w. *In Castle-street, Oxford Market.*

"*Who so fair as lovely Bet?*"

If polished ivory has any resemblance to skin, it may be compared to betsey's, the firmness and smoothness of which are unparallelled: What extasy it is, even to feel so delicate a creature, to one who is an admirer of flesh and blood. Her eyes are blue, and hair of the sandy colour, has extreme good teeth, and a very fine hand and arm: her only fault is being very wide and relaxed in a particular part, which renders her but an indifferent bedfellow if she was not to drink so much tea, (the bane of one third of our females) it would be much the better for her in respect to this relaxation, but women seldom know what is salutary, and generally poison themselves by drams, or throw themselves into confumptions with flip-flops.

Fanny B—tt—n. *Little Saffron-Hill, Hatton Garden*

"*A coal-black joke is here exprefs'd.*"

This girl is one of the blackest haired wenches

wenches in London, with that she has
extreme fine eyes and tolerable teeth,
but her legs are not the beft turned in the
world, fhe is very dextrous in the manual operations, and even when flagel-
lation is required, fhe acquits herfelf to
the entire fatisfaction of her cull, fo that
we may fay, that fhe can turn her hand
to any thing. She has a favourite man
whom fhe fupports, who is upon every
occafion ready to abfent himfelf when a
good man is coming, fo that he may be
ftiled a proper flafh-man. Her price is
eafy, and comes within the compafs of
an angel, unlefs fhe meets a particular
cull, who is fond of fome extraordinary
letch, in this cafe fhe makes them pay
through the nofe, and has at this time a
very artful method of fcrewing the ut-
moft farthing.

Nancy F—rb—k. *In Ely-Court, Hol-*
born.

" *By turns we fing, we dance and play* "

When you fee this little girl, you muft
banifh all forts of cares, for fhe is one of
the liveliest of the age, always dancing,
finging, or romping, fhe hardly gives
herfelf time for her man to enjoy her.
Her perfon is well made, fhe has good
eyes

eyes, and a flat nofe, with very indifferent teeth, well pleafed with a quarter-
guinea.

Sarah C—ll—n. *At a Cabinet-Maker's,
in Wardour ftreet Soho.*

Here is the old fa, ng, " Cut and come again "

A fine firm piece of flefh, good features, hard breaft, and every other part
adequate. The very thing in the winter to thofe who love a fat jolly girl, and
not amifs in the fummer, barring per-
fpiration, Her   , and
ferve to excite the paffion of venery,
even in old age itfelf. Her price is tolerable eafy, and being of a good-natured difpofition, fhe is contented with
almoft any thing.

Nancy D—v—p—t. *At the above-men-
tioned place and conftantly with Sally.*

" But, ye Gods, what a contraft "

This is a villager, and a Yorkfhire gem-
ftone, who feems to keep the other in
awe, diet tests her, and perfuades her
as much as poffible to adopt her notions
of artifice. As her perfon is no way
equal to Sally's, or ftriking in any refpect whatfoever, fhe would, if poffible,
fubftitute a greater fhare of cunning, as
fhe

she thinks, to bring grist to her mill; but all will not do. her method is so infamous, that she is easily seen through: all she gets is very trifling, consequently the comely one is obliged to help her out, by making her partake of that which fortune throws in her way.

Miss Kitty W–ll–s *Broad Court, Bow-street.*

" *None equal plump Kitty for fair skin and*
" *black hair.*"

A good-natured jolly girl, who is always ready to oblige her customers she is fond of a bedfellow, and piques herself upon being a judge of the sports of Venus; loves a bowl of arrack, and never better pleased than when it is going about, for the sake of t'other bowl, rather than be baulked, she would promise you a night's lodging. A piece of gold always contents her if ever so small.

Miss H–wk—s *Charles-street, Marybone.*

" *In her tacit moments she pleases most.*"

Here you may perceive the alehouse-girl in her exalted sphere. After drawing beer, and bringing home the pots for some time, she was taken notice of by one who frequented the house where

the

she lived, and took her into keeping, first trying what mettle she was made of. Soon after this she was forsaken, and left to shift for herself. However, she has a pretty face, fair hair, and blue eyes, about the middling size, and tolerably well made, is really a pretty girl, but so very vulgar in her expressions, that she is only pleasing in bed, when in the act of enjoyment.

Miss Wa—en. *Of the same Place.*
" *'Tis not alone the face I kiss,*
" *The centre part creates my bliss* "

An ordinary piece of stuff, with light hair and blue eyes, ever ready to oblige, let the task be ever so difficult, her manual operations are very great, and by them gets as much money, perhaps, as most of her profession; she has been known to earn her pound per diem, by this single manœuvre. She is not very disagreeable in other respects, being extremely well made in the centre of bliss, whether owing to its being seldomer used than that of prettier women, we will not positively affirm, but it is remarked that the most ordinary girls are generally the best made out of sight. She has no fixt price upon any gentleman's pocket, glad to receive the smallest gratuity.

Miſs Hol—nd. *In New Street, Covent-Garden*

" *Pleaſed to be laughed at for her conceit* "

This lady is a very tall, genteel perſon, very good-natured. and tolerably handſome, dark eyes and hair was debauched by the late Mr. Holland, the Player, whoſe name ſhe bears. She is very fond of ſpouting, and ſeems to have imbibed ſomething of the comedian from her original lover often, in company ſhe has amuſed by her ſpeechifying, and if ſhe does nothing elſe ſhe will ſtand the laugh with good humour Being as eaſy in her price as her temper ſhe is often ſent for, and acquires a tolerable competence.

Miſs Gi—s. *At Mrs. Richardſon's, Bridge's Street.*

" *Inſatiable are the deſires of Gilby.*"

This girl has a very pretty face, fair complexion, and light hair, with dark eyes, about the middle ſize the contraſt of her hair and eyes makes her look very engaging, as, it is our opinion, nothing is more beautiful than black eyes and fair hair. Theſe girls are generally very laſcivious, and are the beſt of bedfellows,

fellows, and, to fay the truth, this girl is
is by no means deficient in this point, for
fhe'd rather go without her fee than be
baulked in the gratification of her paffion :
money here is well laid out, you have
your penny's worth, and of that which
is tolerably good. Half a guinea fatis-
fies her in refpect to cafh, but in point of
venery fhe is fcarce ever contented.

Mifs C—p-r. *Wild-ftreet, Lincolns-Inn-
Fields.*

" *A blafting whore will never thrive* "

Being underfized and infamous are the
only recommendations of this lady. She
has, to be fure, black eyes and hair,
but her blafting method of fpeaking,
were fhe the greateft beauty in London,
would deftroy the whole. What a pity
it is, that girls are fuch fools, as to imagine, that damning, fwearing, and blafting, can poffibly pleafe or entertain !
This is the conftant behaviour of C———r,
otherwife fhe might do extremely well.
Moft girls of this turn come to fome fatal end.

Miſs Ma—ox. *At a Hair-Dreſſer's,
Brownlow Street, Holborn.*

" *Artful ways beguile the implicit rake.*"

A middle-ſized, black-eyed, agreeable
girl, with good dark hair, ever obliging,
and ſeldom out of humour, underſtands
a great deal of her buſineſs, and never
fails to pleaſe. She enjoys her favourite
man with extacy; and pleaſes, with
cold indifference, managed by art, the
reſt of her votaries; who are content in
thinking they have fathomed the deepeſt
part of a girl ſo replete with ſenſation;
in ſhort, ſhe can ſo well counterfeit the
paſſions of love and luſt, that many of the
moſt knowing rakes of the town would
be eaſily deceived. Sometimes ſhe is
lucky enough to receive one pound one,
but in general an angel is her price, and
thanks her ſtars ſhe can get it.

Miſs Th———as. *In New Street, Fetter
Lane.*

" *Good temper, guided by art, ſucceſs muſt
ſurely meet.*"

Never was a girl better calculated for
her buſineſs than this, ſhe is of that complexion which pleaſe many who are particularly fond of red hair, her eyes being

L   ble

blue, and her skin incomparably fair, renders her a very agreeable piece ; add to this a great share of good temper, managed by the art incident to the sex, makes her as complete as any girl of her profession ; she is, also, a very good bed-fellow, and very cleanly, being fond of washing herself, which is very commendable. Half a piece pleases her; but she is apt to give you a hint before hand concerning a present.

Miss Sp—cer. *No. 6, Cumberland Court.*

" *To have it in hand is to be partly sure.*"

An agreeable little girl, not very handsome; fair hair, and tolerable good eyes, what we may call well enough : a very good piece after a good supper and three or four bottles of claret, enjoys what she is about, and expects to be well paid : as to her temper, she is like many others, mighty good humoured when pleased. If you give her a piece of gold, before you enter the premises, she goes to work with great affability and sweetness of temper, but if not, she is cool enough, and thinks of nothing but the money during enjoyment, having suffered much by the bucks of Covent-Garden, she is now very much

upon

upon her guard, and feldom performs before the purfe is drawn out.

Mifs L—we. *At the Turner's, Ruffel Street, Covent Garden*

" *Various modes new defires create.*"

This is an old well experienced woman, or, not to hurt her fame, we will ftill call her girl; loves the fport with an agreeable young fellow who is not foon thrown out. Although marked with the fmall pox, fhe gets a tolerable fhare of money, as fhe ftudies entirely the paffions of men, fhe feldom fails to pleafe, and is generally well paid for what fhe does: nobody underftands Aretine's poftures better than this good lady, and when her lover requires a ftimulator, fhe will contrive fome new pofition, by which fhe can raife to life which otherwife muft have died for want of the thought.

Mifs Pin-ton. *Union Street, Marybone.*

" *Who can refift the charms of youth and beauty.*"

This young lady is really very pretty and very genteel, with brown hair, and as fhe has not been long in this way of life, is very much liked, and in all probability will excel many of her fifterhood,

provided

provided fhe referves herfelf, and ab-
ftains from the lower kind of company.
Being young, and a kind of new face,
fhe is never offered lefs than a guinea,
and, to fay the truth, it is well worth the
money : who would defire youth, beauty
and novelty for lefs?

Mifs Ro--ch.　　*Richmond Street.*

" *Her heart is fixt on one alone.*"

As this lady has not been long upon
the town, it is no wonder fhe is liked,
and, indeed, through her good temper
and her agreeablenefs of perfon, fhe
greatly merits every thing fhe meets
with. A gentleman of Ireland brought
her over, who has now left her; confequently, fhe is obliged to do what, perhaps, goes much againft the grain, and,
as her affection feems to have remained
entirely with this gentleman, every other
becomes indifferent to her, and he muft
be fomething very extraordinary to cap-
tivate her at prefent · fhe now and then
enjoys the man who performs his part
well; but as to its amounting to what
may be called real love, no one can pretend to fay　What fhe does is folely for
what fhe can get; and as fhe underftands
the world, fhe acquires as much as moft
of her profeffion.　　　　　　She

She feems to be endowed with that good
fenfe, that were fhe to meet with fuch
extraordinary luck, the man would be
made happy in a good wife. But as few
women meet with their merit, we fhould
not wonder if fhe continued upon the
town. She well deferves two pounds two,
and indeed is feldom offered lefs.

Sally B—nr—fe. *Eagle-ftreet, Red-lion-
fquare.*

" *Induftry feldom fails.*"

An affable, good-natured girl, brown
hair, good eyes, and tolerable good
teeth; was debauched about a twelve-
month ago by an apothecary's appren-
tice in Holborn. She is indefatigable in
her bufinefs, and acquires, by dint of
great induftry, as much money as moft
girls of her clafs. She is eafily contented, and puts no price upon any perfon's
pocket.

Nancy H—nc—k. *At a Chandler's fhop
in Tothill-ftreet, Weftminfter.*

" *Beauties unfeen can often pleafe.*'

A furprizing girl for wheedling the
men; fhe has fcarce a tooth in her head,
and upon the whole but a very indifferent
perfon, but incomparable fine legs and

L arms,

arms, her hidden charms are greatly fuperior to moſt of her ſex, ſuch an ama-
zing tuft upon *Mount Veneris* would ſur-
prize moſt connoiſſeurs in the female race.
By dint of theſe accompliſhments, (and
let us tell you, no bad ones neither) ſhe
makes her way through life as well as the
beſt of them. Beſides, ſhe can turn her
hand to any thing, and pleaſe the male
creatures without hazarding her conſti-
tution in the leaſt.

Harriet L—be. *At Charlotte H—yes's,
King's-Court, Pall-Mall.*

" *Poſſeſs'd of ev'ry grace, ſhe a better fate
deſerves.*"

This lady is tall, genteel, and reſem-
bles much a girl of ſome faſhion. She
has been greatly in vogue for ſome time,
although we have never taken her into
our liſt. Her hair is very long, and
dreſſes well without any artificial aſſiſtance. The name ſhe bears is that of a
young gentleman ſhe was very fond of
when ſhe lived at Mrs. P-lh-m's, who
kept the ſame houſe ſome years ago.
Upon the whole, ſhe is a very prudent
well-bred girl, much eſteemed by every
one who knows her, and never fails to
pleaſe wherever ſhe is in company. She

is far from the common run of the girls
in her fphere. Her friends are but few,
and fhe feldom goes into company with
any fhe does not know however fhe is
come-at-able, and her price is from two
to five or ten pieces, often having touch-
ed twenty for a night's favor. In fhort,
fhe has got as much money for her time
as any girl in London.

Polly Sm—th *Late of the fame place.*
" *Opportunity once loft, feldom is retrieved.*"

This lady is a very fine girl, dark
eyes and hair, extremely genteel, and
keeps the beft of company. Confiderable offers have been made her, fome of
which fhe has rejected through folly.
Endeavouring to impofe a maiden upon
a gentleman, who offered her 200l. to
fet her up in a milliner's fhop, fhe loft
his friendfhip, and never could reconcile
him to her again, fince which fhe has
rolled on in a middling way, and ferves
as a ftanding difh for the houfe fhe is in.
Two pounds two is about the mark, and
feldom fails to give content. Her method is very engaging, and makes thofe,
who have once had the pleafure of her
acquaintance, fond of embracing every
opportunity of enjoying her company

Miſs G—s.   *In the ſame Court.*

" *In each ſtep a ſuperior grace ſhe ſhews.*"

Gentility and elegance abound with this young lady. Her features are admirably pictured ; and we juſtly may ſay, ſhe has the aſpect of a young lady of faſhion.   Some of the firſt people in England are her conſtant friends, by whom ſhe acquires as much money as any girl at the Weſt-end of the town ; but the expences ſhe is at, and her natural extravagant diſpoſition, cauſes her always to be in arrears, ſo that a couple of pieces are often very acceptable.

Sally P—w—l.   *At the Coal-ſhed in Wych-ſtreet.*

" *The hypocrite will ſure, &c.* "

This poor girl is a moſt indefatigable piece of ſtuff ; her perſon is rather tall, her face is nothing extraordinary, but by dint of a good tongue ſhe can do much when ſhe finds a man of a good-natured diſpoſition, and fond of hearing her talk, ſhe will enter upon the topic of religion, and give you an account of the reformation, pronouncing herſelf a ſtrong papiſt, pleading her great diſtreſs for the life ſhe leads, and by theſe means wheedles

dles a man out of half a guinea, when perhaps he would not have given her half as much. The plaintive, religious whore often prevails over a weak mind, and excites a man's compassion.

Polly D—x—n. *In Brook-street.*

" *Globular forms to some are pleasing.*"

A sturdy wench, with great breasts, good eyes, good teeth, always ready to oblige, and an extraordinary good bed-fellow.

Sally Str—on. *At a Grocer's in Little Wild-street.*

" *Nor bars nor turnpikes shall my way impede.*"

The character of this lady is very singular, having been upon the town near six months without ever having been fairly entered. She is so conformed as to require a peculiar method of cohabiting with her, a bar being naturally in the way, which causes a kind of obstruction, without fixing her in a certain position, no one can perform what he would wish to do. Her face is extremely agreeable, good eyes, fine teeth, about the middling size, and inclinable to be fat. She might easily pass for a maiden-

head,

head, if fhe kept her own fecrets; but fhe feems to be too honeft, or rather too fimple to deceive any one in that particular. Her price is optional, confequently every thing is made very eafy, excepting her commodity.

Sukey P—ll—ngt—n. *Lived lately at an Earthen-ware Shop in Holborn, to be found in the 2s. Gallery, right hand fide.*

" *The decree of Fate muft here take place.*"

This young lady has not been in this way of life above two months, ran away from her father, a clergyman about 20 miles off, after an officer who debauched her, when fhe came to town, after feeing him two or three times, he forfook her, and went to Ireland to join his regiment; in confequence of which, being afhamed to return home, fhe was obliged to throw herfelf upon the town. She is a fine girl, about 18 years old, light brown hair, and very agreeable features, of the middling fize, extremely fenfible, but owns her folly in preferring a red coat Her paffions are ftill dormant, or rather fixed in her feducer; however fhe is an agreeable companion, and deferves a better fate. One pound one is what fhe expects.

Dolly

Dolly N–fb—t.   *In Fetter-Lane, near*
Holborn , to be met with in the upper Boxes.

" By falfe pretences dupes are led afiray "

A plump little piece, with good dark
eyes and hair, incomparable fine teeth,
and a quantity of fmall talk; has not
been in town above four or five months;
but carried on fome bufinefs of the fame
kind at Poitfmouth, under another name.
If you afk her any queftions relative to
her being in this way, fhe will tell you
fhe was debauched about fix months ago,
and never was at Portfmouth in her life;
but, from fome officers being carnally
concerned with her, we may venture to
affirm it for truth.   Upon the ftrength
of her imagining herfelf to be believed,
fhe expects a good price.

Nancy F–rt—cue.   *Marybone-ftreet, Pic-*
cadilly, to be heard of at the Cat in the
Strand

" The choleric are dangerous companions."

A little Welch paffionate girl, about
22, good eyes and teeth, with a ruddy
complexion, no body's enemy but her
own, piques herfelf upon her Welch
blood, the effects of which are very often fatal, whether partly affectation or
not,

not, we won't pretend to determine.
As her country in general are paffionate,
we are apt to impute it to her native air.
Bottles, glaffes, &c. unexpectedly will
fly at your head, if you give her the leaft
provocation, and has often loft her a
good friend. She bears no malice, it is
true, for in lefs than five minutes fhe
will fight, laugh, and cry, but the latter very often too late. Half a guinea
is her price, but take care you pay her,
or woe betide you.

Mrs. H——g. *No* 22, *Rathbone-Place,*
Oxford-Road.

" *In vain for youth we all may contend,*
" *Age to beauty will foon put an end.*"

This lady was born of a good family
in Lincolnfhire; but, being naturally of
a froward difpofition, fhe found means
to deceive her parents, and made her
efcape to London with a young Hibernian, who feeking out the natural bent
of her inclinations, foon found an eafy
accefs to the fortrefs he had long been
waiting to ftorm, but her father dying
foon afterwards my young gentleman
was difappointed in his hopes of poffeffing
any fortune at his deceafe, and therefore
foon gave her an opportunity to feek for
another

another keeper, which was one M..
H——g, a tobacconift, whofe name fhe
now affumes. She lived with him as his
wife for many years : he dying, fhe was
again left to fhift for herfelf, but, with
prudence and induftry, fhe foon acquired
money fufficient to furnifh her a houfe,
which fhe now lets out to ladies of her
own ftamp; fo that what by furnifhing
gentlemen with young tit bits when ne-
ceffity requires, and by trading (old as
fhe is) a little in her own way, fhe has
at length gained a comfortable livelihood.

Mrs. H——g is a genteel fair woman,
has light hair, blue eyes, and neat an-
cles, fhe is about the age of 40, though
fhe feldom owns herfelf above 25, remarkable for her amorous difpofition,
and earneft defire to pleafe her cuftomers, whom fhe would rather treat in
her turn, than part without being both
mutually fatisfied.—*the following anecdote
concerning her is absolutely a fact*. Two
young *bucks* went home and flept with
her all night, early in the morning they
pretended bufinefs out of town, and each
flipt fomething in her hand at parting.
When fhe arofe to breakfaft, anxious to
ook at her prize, expecting two guinea:

M   a

at leaft, to her great fhame and difa-
pointment, fhe found only *two bad half-
pence.*

Mifs W—ms. *At a Watch-makers, Noel-
ftreet, Soho.*

" *Virtue is the fureft guide.*"

This lady was the daughter of an eminent farmer in South Wales, who fent
her to London very young, to be under
the care of an old aunt, with whom fhe
had not long refided before a young
gentleman ingratiated himfelf fo far in
her good graces, as to gain her confent
to make *him* happy by her ruin, under a
promife of marriage—but no fooner had
enjoyment damped the ardour of his
love, than he abandoned her to the re-
proaches and calumny of a mercilefs
world, 'till at length with fhame and
difappointment fhe quitted her aunt's, and
entered on the town in the fixteenth
year of her age.

We have nothing to fay concerning
this lady's character no more than this,
if fhe had not quitted the paths of virtue
fhe might have proved an honour and an
ornament to her fex, as fhe is poffeffed
of every good and amiable quality to
make this affertion true.

Miſs W——ms is rather ſhort and fat, has a fine clear ſkin—her face altogether, tho' not beautiful is very agreeable, with the addition of fine eyes and a good ſet of teeth,—ſhe is at preſent in keeping by Mr. B——, her cuſtomers, whenever inclined to pay her a viſit, are always ſure to be received with a behaviour and politeneſs becoming a perſon in a higher ſtation.

Miſs H——n   No. 54, Newman-ſtreet.
" *The ſize of her parts due proportion bear.* "

This lady is of a Patagonian ſize, has a remarkable clear ſkin, fine hair, black eyes, and good teeth. She was daughter of a late Captain E——ot, and lives at preſent with the ſon of an eminent cabinet maker in Greek-ſtreet, but being out of his power to lay any reſtriction on her conduct as he pleaſes, (not being able at preſent to ſupport her himſelf) ſhe is obliged to have recourſe to others for a maintainance. ſhe is a woman of no ſort of breeding, unleſs vulgar expreſſions may be termed ſuch, and ſeldom meets with any encouragement but from thoſe who are fond of Billingſgate language— as her ſize is large, ſo by the addition of a high head dreſs, ſhe endeavours to ren-

M 2   der

der herself ridiculous to those who would otherwise admire her as a fine woman.

Miss P-tt. *At a Chandler's shop, Langley-street, Long-acre.*

" *Lost to every sense of shame,*
" *Her mates declare her well known fame.*"

This lady is too well known about the Garden to need any description, it is really very surprifing that a girl as *she is,* possessed of a decent sum of money when of age, should thus injure her reputation by keeping company with the common vagrants and pick-pockets under the Piazza —She is very rarely sent for into company, unless to amuse them with her natural sprightly turn of wit and uncommon pertness of behaviour.

Miss R—rds. *At the Cook's shop, Princes street.*

" *Her bread depends upon her walks by night.*"

This lady tho' sprung from a low beginning, by keeping good company has made herself respected by all her admirers, she is rather short, but lusty, a little marked with the small pox, and is well known by her nocturnal walks thro' the Hay market and Coventry ftreet

Miſs Ne—t. *At the Hardware ſhop, King-ſtreet, Weſtminſter.*

" *The deportment of the fair is ſure to pleaſe.*"

This lady was the daughter of a glazier in the Borough, and is very remarkable for her fine ſlender ſhape, ſhe is about the age of thirty, yet with the addition of a little **red** and white ſhe makes herſelf paſs tolerably well for ſixteen. She has been a fair girl, but time and intemperance have raiſed a few furrows on her brow, notwithſtanding ſhe is ſtill admired for her genteel addreſs and behaviour.

Miſs L—s *Crown ſtreet, Weſtminſter.*

" *Like Ophelia ſhe mourns the fatal loſs.*"

This lady's caſe is truly pitiable, as ſhe has ſome months ago loſt a kind and tender keeper, which has almoſt brought her to a degree of madneſs, as is evident by her behaviour in going every night and ſtrewing flowers over his grave.—She is about five and twenty, rather tall and genteel, brown complexion, dark eyes, and modeſt countenance, yet grief and vexation has rendered her quite the reverſe from what ſhe formerly was,

Miſs

Miss Co—ton. *Crown-court, Chancery-lane.*

" *So fair, and yet so foul a mouth we have not seen.*"

A tall genteel girl, remarkably fair and tolerably handsome, but her vulgar behaviour eclipses all her other charms: she has very few admirers owing to her strong attachment to *gentlemen of the comb,* she is however said to give great satisfaction to her favourite votries.

Fanny B—en. *Queen-street, Broad-way, Westminster.*

" *O ! Parents, consider the child in futuro.*"

This is a decent, well-bred, young lady, about twenty two, was brought up in a convent at Boulogne, her father being a man who had an extreme good place for life, during which period he could very well afford to bring her up in the way he did, but being too ambitious to have her upon the haut ton was the cause of her ruin, after his decease she was left to the wide world to shift for herself, her mother dying when she was very young. Which way to turn herself she knew not : the whole of the father's effects went to pay some debts, so that being totally

out

out of subsistance, she applied to one of those handy old women, who oblige gentlemen with the newest ware, an opportunity which to her seemed the dernier resource, consequently was resolved to embrace it · in short after loosing her maidenhead for a trifling consideration, she was obliged to commence trader, and has for some time past obtained a decent livelihood. She is a very elegant, genteel fair girl, light hair, and extreme fine skin, is often to be seen in the boxes; her price is from two to five guineas.

Miss Al-f-n. *At a grocer's shop, in Green street, Grosvenor square.*

" *Tho' so slim and so thin,*
" *I should like to be akin.*"

A lady about twenty seven years of age, elegant in her deportment, tall and thin, good eyes, and longish nose—on the point of taking a house upon her own bottom, backed by a particular friend who is to advance her a sum for that purpose: she was kept by a Norfolk gentleman who has settled thirty pounds a year upon her; but provisions &c. being dear she for these twelve months has picked up a little cash in our way. By

giving

giving her timely notice you may be accommodated with her charms at the reafonable price of one pound one.

Sally F—m—n *At a Chandler's fhop, Fleet market.*

" *Take heed how you embark.*"

This *delicate* lady is to be met with between Temple-bar and the place of her abode, fhe fets fail betwen the hours of feven and eight, if fhe meets with any captures fhe generally fets fire to them, and bears away with what plunder fhe can conveniently carry off. She is Dutch built, broad bottomed, and carries a great deal of fail. Goods put on board her reafonably fraited.

Kitty F—d—e. *Near the Pantheon, Oxford ftreet.*

" *Education is the refinement of manners.*"

This young lady was a Clergyman's daughter of Bedfordfhire : her real name being Wells, but in confequence of a connexion fhe had with fome perfon of the fame name fhe now bears, fhe thught proper to change her own : fhe is a very pretty thick girl, tolerably god teeth, and fine neck and breafts : her acquaintance are of the bettermoft
fort,

fort, and unlefs fhe has fome kind of knowledge of you it is rather difficult to engage with her, however, by dint of a fmall fhare of affiduity, you may find a way to her moft fecret apartment. As her education is far fuperior to the generality of the girls of her ftamp, fhe expects to be treated accordingly, fometimes a piece of paper is what fhe expects, but in general a couple of pieces is the ftandard.

Nancy S—ks Next door to the Blue Pofts, Charing Crofs

" *No beauty here is to be found* "

This is a brown girl of the middling fize, black eyes, dark hair and extremely good humoured, it is true, fhe has no great pretenfions to beauty, but is one of thofe unhappy fair ones, who was forfaken by her friends, upon her firft falfe ftep. fhe is upon the whole a poor unhappy girl, and deferves a better fate Eafy enough of accefs, her price being any thing in reafon

Betfy M-l-s. At a Cabinet maker's, Oldftreet, Clerkenwell.

" *Which way you will and pleafe you.* "

Known in this quarter for her immenfe fize!

fized breafts, which fhe alternately makes ufe of with the reft of her parts, to indulge thofe who are particularly fond of a certain amufement. She is what you may call, at all, backwards and forewards, are all equal to her, pofteriors not excepted, nay indeed, by her own account fhe has moft pleafure in the latter. Very fit for a foreign Macaroni—entrance at the front door tolerably reafonable, but nothing lefs then two pound two for the back way. As her perfon has nothing remarkable one way or the other, we fhall leave her for thofe of the Italian gufto.

Polly H—t.　*In Titchfield ftreet, Newport market.*

" *A conflagration difficult to extinguifh.*"

The paffions of this lady are inordinate, or what may go under the appellatum of that unhappy diforder, called a furor uterinus. She is never fatisfied let who will be her bedfellow conteqⁿntly can refufe no man, not confidering at the fame time her own intereft, if you give her any thing its very well if not, it is the fame and you may return again. Her perfon is really agreeable, being tall and well made, with remarkable

good

goodlegs If a man wants a good bed-fellow, she is very well for one night, and as we have said before, she has no price upon any man's pocket.

Charlotte G—sb—r—gh. Lambeth marsh.
" *On her back she motionless lays.*"

A genteel fancy piece without any meaning, a perfect still life, neither any thing to say, or scarce any thing to do, she is motionless in the very height of the sport, preferring rather a pinch of snuff to all the joys of venery. She has tolerable good eyes and teeth, and not a bad skin, as a picture she is well enough and deserves to be paid accordingly.

Miss Emelia S—ot. At a Shoe maker's, in Westminster. To be seen in the two shilling gallery right hand side.
" *Be cautious, ye fair, of the man you trust.*"

A good pretty Scotch lass about eighteen, strong features, black hair, and eyes, with extraordinary good teeth. She was debauched by a Scotch gentleman in the army; but finding an opportunity to marry, he left her with a small present, promising her great things when he came into his wife's fortune, which was said to be considerable;

but

but as this proved only a pretence to get rid of her, she was obliged to shift for herself and make the most of her person: she has some extraordinary good acquaintance, and does as well as most of her sisterhood.

Betsy C—k—r—n. At Mrs. Holmes, Air street, Piccadilly.

"*Vain of nature's gifts, bespeak the weakness of the mind.*"

This young lady may with justice be said to be an extraordinary piece in her way, she resembles much the woman of fashion. Her hair is of a beautiful flaxen colour, eyes blue, and shape elegant, there is a certain ease about her which renders her truly amiable. The only fault she is possessed of, is her vanity, which is almost insufferable; but fine women will give themselves airs. A bank note is not thought much of, her usual price being five pieces,

Eleanor C—y. In Silver street, Golden-square.

" *Artificial virginry answers every end* "

A plump little girl, with good eyes, and indifferent teeth, firm breasts, and fit for those who love a tight piece, having

ing paffed feveral times for a maidenhead, by the help of a little art the fex
are acquainted with, fuch as alum water
&c. fhe has fold this commodity a dozen
times, within thefe five months, and has
been well paid for the fame. An old
matron is her conductor, and introduces
her where fhe thinks the man can eafily
be duped. A practice very common in
London, and as furprifing that men are
fuch fools.

Fanny M–n—th. *No.* 15, *Ruffel Street.*
" *Judge not by outward forms.*"

A pretty young girl about nineteen,
refembling a Quaker in her drefs, or
rather a wolf in fheeps cloathing, her
features are regular and pretty, of a fair
complexion. She was debauched by a
defigning young fellow, who was fervant
to a Nobleman, and after having gratified his paffion with her, he with great
artifice found means to introduce her to
his mafter, for a maidenhead, by which
means he received a gratuity and got rid
of a girl who would in all probability
have proved very troublefome to him,
being apprehenfive of her being with
child. His lordfhip was foon tired of
her, made her a prefent and difcharged

N   her

her; after which she was forced to take to the busine∫s she now follows, and is contented with the smalle∫t piece of gold.

Nancy C—∫t—er. *In Orange Street, oppo∫ite Long-court.*

" *Guard again∫t the wor∫t.*"

This girl is remarkably thin in the face, long no∫e, and very indifferent features, has extreme good legs, and ∫omething el∫e that mu∫t plea∫e the ∫en∫ation pro tempore, but we wont pretend to an∫wer for any con∫equence in futuro, as ∫he has a good deal of bu∫ine∫s in the ∫mall and nocturnal way. Her terms are rea∫onable, and ∫he is very well plea∫ed with a quarter guinea.

Mi∫s D-r—r *At Mrs. Smith's, in Ru∫∫el Street, Bloom∫bury.*

" *Youth, here you may ∫ee in its purity* "

This young lady has not been debauched above two months, by an Officer of the guards, who at pre∫ent keeps her company; but having had many importunities, at length ∫he broke the vow of continence and gave up her charms to a certain Jew in the city, who made her a very genteel pre∫ent, and has ∫ince
often

often vifited her in the abfence of the Captain, whofe allowance being far from fufficient to maintain her, fhe is obliged to make it out by private connexions. She is a remarkable fprightly girl, about eighteen, brown hair, and dark eyes, fings a good fong, and is in fhort an agreeable companion. Her expectations are rather exorbitant, being fpoilt by the Jew's lavifh manner of treating her, however, it is fuppofed fhe will know the value of money better foon and be fatisfied with a couple of pieces.

Mifs H–ll. At Mrs. Fl——g's, alias Mrs. H—l—n, mentioned in this lift, in Rathbone place

" By bulying three's fhe extorts the gol "

She is rather fhort, but has pleafing regular features, a good auburn hair, and a fine fkin. Altho' not twenty years of age, fhe is an adept at her bufinefs, and underftands not only the art of fleecing, but alfo the art of bullying her vifitors. If you prefent her with what they call a *whore's curfe*, fhe *damns* you for the compliment, half a piece foftens the tone of her voice, and makes her attempt to pleafe by a fong. But a

N 2   guinea

guinea makes her the goddess of every thing desireable, the only disagreeable thing which attends her, are her teeth, which for want of cleaning, become very often offensive, especially if a rampant young fellow happens to tip her the velvet.

Miss Da—el. *At the same place.*

" *By compliant ways we ever please,*
" *And always set the mind at ease.*"

This lady is also of the middle size, very fair, and her hair is inclined to be classical She is a good-natured, easy, complaisant girl, she takes what you give her, and receives it with a cheerful heart· in short she attempts to please, and seems to be happy if she succeeds· propose what you will she will with great condescension come into it, never saying no to any thing Her price is tolerably easy being very well pleased with half a guinea or even a quarter guinea.

Miss Clare H—y—rd. *At Mrs.* B—k's *in Curson Street, May-fair.*

" *Competence should always the mind content.*"

A favourite of Mrs. B—k's, being always upon the spot and very attentive to business, the best milch-cow she has.
She

She is a fine girl about twenty two, good hair, eyes and teeth, and loves a chearful glafs, her favourite is a gentleman of fortune, through whofe affiftance fhe might live tolerably; but being never contented and at a great expence for board, cloaths &c. fhe is in a manner obliged to admit of other fuitors and indeed with them can fcarce keep out of debt, the good lady of the houfe taking great care to fcrew her down to the laft farthing, charging exorbitantly for board and lodging, even her wafherwoman charges her double for every thing, as fhe does the reft of her fifterhood. We fhould be glad to know if a girl fhould not contrive to live upon fix or eight guineas a week, without running in debt? but they being fo terribly taxed is the reafon they can fcarce make both ends meet.

Mifs Sally H—fon. *At the fame place.*
" *Softer than the bed of down her bofom proves.*"

A fit perfon to grace a table, being very fat and comely, a good winter piece, and indeed upon the whole not difagreeable. Her features are pleafing, good teeth, and not deficient in point of

N 3 fenfe,

fenfe, if her lovers tell truth, nor even in fenfation, for fhe is faid to be very fond of the fport. Her footing is rather fuperior to the common run and expects five pieces, but being often difappointed is very well pleafed with two or three.

Mrs. C-x. Alfo at the fame place.

" *If parts can conquer great and fmall.*
" *Sure — — — and Cox muft needs do all.*"

This lady is a kind of boatfwain in her way, and when fhe fpeaks, every thing fhe fays is uttered with a thundering and vociferous tone. Her particular acquaintance is a Scotch Officer who plays upon the bagpipes, whether he fancies her voice is a kind of double bafs or not, we wont pretend to fay, but that he feems to be extremely fond of her is moft certain. Her perfon is agreeable enough, her features ftriking, and altogether a tolerable good piece. We apprehend this lady would be an extraordinary good companion for a fea Officer, as fhe might fave him fome trouble in giving the word. This lady is the firft female Champion for Englifh liberty, Mrs. M—c—ly not excepted, the hiftorian being only an advocate in Theory, whilft Mrs. C-x has ftood forth in
perfon

perfon and compelled the martial mafter
of the ceremonies at the Pantheon, to
yield to the rights of beauty and the
Britifh fair.

Betfy S—ven—n.   *In Newman Street.*
    " *Fond fhe is and e'er will be,*
    " *Of a King's new good guinea.*"

Juft returned from Margate, where
fhe has wafhed away all the impurities
of proftitution, and rifen almoft imma-
culate like Venus from the waves. If
the fpring and even the fummer of her
beauty be paft, fhe is not without hopes
of a fruitful autumn. This lady is rather
above the middle fize, inclined to the
embon point, of a fair complexion, and
the feat of blifs is beyond all defcription.

Mifs W—lls.   *At the bow window, Park-
lane.*

    " *With the fports of the field, here's no
        pleafure can vie*
    " *Then follow, follow, &c. the hounds in full
        cry* "

A fine tall girl, about 25, elegant in
perfon, with a captivating countenance.
She has found out the true art to pleafe
and be pieafed. Mifs W—lls has tafted
the fweets of many good things in purfe
                                        and

and perfon, and relifhes them all. Her predominant paffion however feems for horfes, hounds, and the delights of the field. No one is more emulous than our heroine to be in at the death: upon the whole we may pronounce this lady a woman of tafte and fpirit, which fhe difplays in nothing more forcibly, hunting not excepted, than in the choice of her favourite as he is ftill a hunter.

Mifs S—w. Charles Street, Covent Garden.
To be feen in the galleries at the play-houfes.

" *Lover's hearts are not their own hearts,*
" *Nor lungs, nor lights and fo forth downwards.*"

The witty Butler has thus ludicroufly defcribed the fituation of a male lover, and with a fmall addition it is very applicable to Mifs S—w, for all her parts have long fince been the property of the town. Though fhe is a profeft woman of pleafure, fhe feems to do nothing for her own amufement but for intereft and the Doctors emolument. We fhall therefore add no farther defcription but refer to the place of her abode, that fhe may be fhunned.

Nancy

Nancy T—l-r   *At Mrs. S—tt—n's,*
Charles ſtreet, Covent Garden.

" Deform'd by Nature, yet to Vice inclin'd."

This is a piece of proſtituted deformity. girls upon our liſt need never deſpair making their way, if ſuch a poor unhappy creature as this can any how live. She has neither make nor ſize, being what is generally called broken backed, with a ſmall face and longiſh noſe, her eyes, indeed, are tolerable, her legs long and thin, and ſeems as if they were hung on with wires However her good humour and condeſcenſion makes up for many deformities, and upon the whole ſhe keeps pidling on and juſt makes a livelihood,

Betſy J—nn—gs.   *At a Chandler's ſhop,*
in Oxford ſtreet.

" Let the preſent hour be mine."

A pompous heroic girl, without either wit or humour, but fancies herſelf clever without any perſon acquieſcing with her whomſoever. She is of the red-haired kind and very vicious, too fond of the male kind for her buſineſs, which is the cauſe of her not ſucceeding as ſhe ſhould do. Her perſon is extremely well made, good eyes, fair ſkin, and incomparable

fine

fine hair, never fo happy as when in
bed with a pretty fellow, altho' fhe gets
nothing by him—like the giddy girl,
thinks of nothing but the prefent, leaving all future events to chance. She
left an elderly man, who would have
given her five guineas, to bed with a
young fellow who had not a fingle fix-
pence, and having herfelf juft one guinea
thought it fufficient to defray the expence of the night and the following
day, leaving herfelf without a farthing
for the fake of a few hours indulgence
with this favourite. Whatever money
fhe receives from her indifferent cuftomers, fhe holds in a kind of contempt,
and longs for an opportunity to throw it
away upon her favorite man—generally
one who is pennylefs and glad of even a
dinner.

Dolly H—t—y. *Blenheim ftreet, Marl-
borough Mewfe.*

" *Hit or mifs, luck's all* "

A black little girl, with good eyes and
good teeth, was kept fome time fince
by a tradefman, who has fince failed and
took the benefit of the laft infolvent act.
Being upon the commons during that
period, fhe has been obliged to do as
well

well as fhe can. She takes her evening walks to the play-houfes and the piazza, where fhe often, before fhe returns home, makes her half guinea, fometimes a pound. She is one of thofe who turn their hand to any thing: fhe performs the manual operation as well as any of her profeffion, Her price is what fhe can get,

Mifs R——n——w Cold Bath fields, to be often feen at Bagnigge Wells in the fummer, and in the Play-houfe galleries in the winter.

" *The wh——re with prudence earns her bread* "

This lady makes a point of never carrying any perfon home with her, pretending the modefty of the houfe where fhe lives, fhe generally is lucky enough to ftay out two or three times a week, and indeed when fhe comes home often has met with flyer or two which fecures a good half guinea. Sometimes fhe meets with an old codger who gives her a guinea for her trouble exclufive of the rods. They meet at a certain Tavern once a week, where he is well known for the flogging cull. The waiters of the houfe have often, through peep-holes,

holes, been witnefs to very extraordinary fcenes, which have paft between this couple. She places this debilitated cull, among the beft of her cuftomers, and upon the whole fhe gets a great deal of money for a woman in her way; fhe manages her bufinefs with fo much art, that fhe paffes for a widow in the neighbourhood where fhe lives, who lives upon her fortune.

Peggy D—l—d. *Great Poulteney Street, Golden fquare.*

" *At an eafy price you may here feaft well.*"

This lady takes her name from a gentleman of that name who debauched her, and has fince left her to fhift for herfelf, without making any provifion for her, not even giving her enough to pay the lodging fhe was in at that time. fhe may be faid to be a good-natured, agreeable girl, about 20 , fair hair and fkin, with tolerable good teeth , in fhort fhe's a good piece. A man may indulge here very well at the eafy rate of half a guinea.

T H E E N D.